The Commandments of Jesus Christ

According to the Gospel of Matthew

The writer of **The Commandments of Jesus Christ** takes an in-depth look at the words spoken by Jesus Christ according to the Gospel of Matthew.

What makes this book exceptional is that no quotes of any other writer outside the Bible are used on the subjects that Jesus spoke about. To illuminate any of the subjects that Jesus taught, only cross references to other sections of the Bible are made.

This book is an illuminating and honest study of the teachings of Jesus by a sincere and diligent student of the Bible.

Jesus Christ is the Savior of the world, the long-awaited Messiah. Are you brave enough to listen and do what He came to reveal to this world during His short ministry on earth?

God send His only Son to earth with messages from Him to clarify His will, His character and His purpose with the human race. Are you interested?

Then this book is a must-read for you.

The Commandments of Jesus Christ
According to the Gospel of Matthew

S. E. Botha

First published
2018

Layout
Hanánja Dreyer

Editors
Rebecca Joubert
André Joubert

Contents

Prologue i
Chapter 1: The Sermon on the Mount 1
Chapter 2: Educating the disciples 50
Chapter 3: Teaching through parables 78
Chapter 4: Jesus answers trick questions 108
Chapter 5: Comments on the Scribes and Pharisees 153
Chapter 6: Predicting the future 162
Chapter 7: Important short quotes and statements spoken by Jesus 189
Annexure A: A Biblical view of the state of the dead 203

Tables:

Table 1	Opposite meaning of words	4
Table 2	Definition of those to whom the Kingdom of Heaven belongs	5
Table 3	Characteristic and promise	7
Table 4	Light versus Darkness	34
Table 5	Main themes of the parables	106
Table 6	Explanation of related parables	146
Table 7	Basis for condemnation of Scribes and Pharisees	159
Table 8	Signs to look out for: the Destruction of Jerusalem and the End of the World	164
Table 9	The meaning of the different entities in the parable of the ten virgins	172

Prologue

Are the Commandments of Jesus Christ a contradiction in terms? Not if you believe that Jesus Christ is the Son of God and that He came to earth with a calling and a ministry.

According to Matthew 28 Jesus said, *"and teach them everything that I have commanded you"*. And yes, it is true that these words can be translated to sound more consumer friendly in the modern translations, but the fact remains: The words that Jesus spoke when He came to earth are of utmost importance for everyone who is hungry to hear the very words of God. In the first place it is important that we understand His words, but His words should also have an impact on our attitudes and especially our behavior.[1] If we do not practice that which Jesus taught we cannot be Christians in the real sense of the word, or in His own words:

> *"Whosoever therefore shall break one of these least commandments, and shall teach men so, he shall be called the least in the kingdom of heaven"* (Matt.5:19).

Yes, He had a calling to come to earth to pay the ransom for our sins - yours and mine – on the cross – so that whoever believes in Him as their personal Savior shall have eternal life.[2] Yet, He also had a

---

[1] John 3:36
[2] John 3:16

ministry when He came to earth – to live a life without sinning, delivering service to the people and teaching messages from his Father. The main purpose was to set the record straight. People misinterpreted God's Word, His character and His will. Jesus came to practically demonstrate the true nature of God - to tell them about the really important issues concerning the Kingdom of heaven.

As it was put in Mark 10:45

"For even the Son of man came not to be ministered unto, but to minister, and to give his life a ransom for many."

Are we intimidated by our churches' doctrines (the traditions of men) or our own ideas to such an extent that the clear words of Jesus have become vague or distant? Pray that the Holy Spirit will open your mind and your heart to be able to grasp the truth spoken so clearly by Jesus Christ. In Matthew 24 where Jesus spoke about the future He warned His disciples three times against false teaching (verse 4), false prophets (verse 11) and false Christs and prophets (verse 24).

The red letter edition of the New Testament makes it easy to follow every word that Jesus spoke. It is thus relatively easy to determine that He sometimes spoke in ordinary conversation, sometimes He used just one sentence loaded with wisdom (quotes) and at other occasions He deliberately taught His disciples through parables and sermons.

For the purpose of this book the focus will be on **the teachings of Jesus** as portrayed mainly in the **Gospel of Matthew**, with cross references to the other Gospels and other books of the Bible when needed to illuminate or expand on a thought. Let us put aside for the moment all the writings of theologians, priests, pastors and saints and concentrate on the Bible alone for its interpretation.

It might be a good idea to read this book through the first time, and then read it slowly a second time, looking up each cross reference in the footnotes, using your favorite Bible. If you are worried that a text is taken out of context, by all means read the whole chapter to which the verse refers to, or the whole book in the Bible. And if you the reader think the Bible text in the foot note does not correspond with the idea in the text, please communicate this to the writer. The e-mail address is: jonksda@gmail.com. If you differ from the writer on any matter please refrain from quoting other writers, but give proof of your view by quoting from the Bible alone. The question is: can you and I handle the truth as spoken by Jesus Christ, or are we stuck in a certain way of thinking. We as Christians believe that the Holy Spirit will guide us in interpreting and understanding the Bible. If we differ greatly on a subject, we have to come to the conclusion that one of us, or both, are not listening to the guidance of the Holy Spirit.

Please take note that sometimes the numbering of verses in, for example the book of Psalms, differ in different translations.

The emphasis will be on the direct teachings of Jesus as portrayed in His major discourses as found in:

- The Sermon on the Mount (Matthew 5 – 7)
- The discourse on discipleship (Matthew 10, 11 12)
- Teaching through parables (Matthew 13)
- Jesus answers trick questions (Matthew 15-22)
- Comments on the scribes and Pharisees (Matthew 23)
- Predicting the future (Matthew 24 - 26)
- Short quotes and statements

Jesus taught us by *the example* He set. He was baptized. He had compassion for his fellow human beings as He relieved their physical and emotional pain. He gathered a core group to train and established sincere relationships with them. For every need He was dependent on His Father and the Holy Spirit.[3] He did not invest in earthly treasures. He kept the Ten Commandments in the way His Father wanted it to be kept and not as the Pharisees preached. In no way was He sheltered or protected from the emotional traumas of life, for instance the trauma of eventually separating from

---

[3] Joh.14:21,25,26,28

the people that He had grown to love in a very personal way. Ultimately, He was obedient to His Father, even unto death. His acts speak of His unfailing integrity, never wavering from his principles or life goal.

For the purpose of this study however, we are specifically interested in what *Jesus taught*. In Matthew 28 He mentioned that his disciples should teach the people to *"observe all things that I have commanded you"*. What are these? They are found in the Sermon on the Mount, yes, and during many other occasions when Jesus actively set out to teach the disciples certain principles to govern the way they should live and work even after His death. The points He wanted to stress were often illustrated through parables.

One of the main themes that Jesus was trying to get across was that our emphasis in life should be on spiritual matters more than material matters. Thus He often introduced a teaching or parable referring to the kingdom of heaven/God.

True Christians do not need theologians, priests or ministers to interpret the words and teachings of Jesus to them for they are simple to grasp. If we pray for God's assistance, for Him to send us his Holy Spirit to help us understand and interpret his Word, we will be successful.[4] Understanding the Bible can be described in terms of *levels of*

---

[4] 1 Cor.2:13

understanding. Reading a verse containing some of the instructions of Jesus just on a superficial level, usually sounds quite pleasing to the ear, but we should study every verse within its context. We should also not be afraid to dig a little deeper – as for hidden treasure and also compare a text with other texts of the Bible on the same subject, to enable us to grasp the full meaning.

The writer refrained from quoting directly from other sections of the Old or New Testament to save space, but included such references as footnotes, especially for the more serious Bible student. The King James Version of the Bible was used.

And yes, Jesus' instructions are meant to be followed, and to be obeyed.[5] They are not to be seen as soothing greeting card words – just to read and forget. That is why the title of this book is "The Commandments of Jesus Christ" – it is meant as a wake-up call for Christians.

The fact is: do you believe that Jesus Christ came to earth as the Son of God to become the Son of Man[6] and to die for your sins? Really? Then you should take every word spoken by this Man in a more serious light, because according to His own words He is coming to this earth again, and next time not as a lamb to be slain. No, next time, He will

---

[5] Joh.15:14
[6] Matt.8:20; 9:6;10:23; 11:19; 12:8; 26:2,24,45,64; Rev.1:13; 14:14

be sitting on a throne to judge the world and separate the goats and the sheep (Matthew 25).

We are so used to hearing smooth talkers that the plain truth spoken by Jesus will sometimes be hard for us to bear. Are the Gospels only about Good News? Are we deaf to truths that we do not like? Open your ears and investigate with me. Let's give Jesus a chance to speak to us.

Are the commandments of Jesus Christ different from the commandments of the Old Testament? Jesus validated the Old Testament and according to Matthew, Jesus quoted from: Isaiah, Micah, Hosea, Jeremiah, Deuteronomy, Psalms, Exodus, Leviticus, Malachi, Genesis, Zechariah, Daniel.

Back to the Bible, yes let's investigate the Gospel of Matthew to hear and understand what Jesus Christ came to tell us and even more: to live by these principles.

Chapter 1

Sermon on the Mount

The first major teachings of Jesus, according to Matthew, can be found in **Matthew 5**, known as the **Sermon on the Mount**, because it was delivered on a mountainside in Galilee.

> "[3]*Blessed are the poor in spirit: for theirs is the kingdom of heaven.* [4]*Blessed are they that mourn: for they shall be comforted.* [5]*Blessed are the meek: for they shall inherit the earth.* [6]*Blessed are they which do hunger and thirst after righteousness: for they shall be filled.* [7]*Blessed are the merciful: for they shall obtain mercy.* [8]*Blessed are the pure in heart: for they shall see God.* [9]*Blessed are the peacemakers: for they shall be called the children of God.* [10]*Blessed are they which are persecuted for righteousness' sake: for theirs is the kingdom of heaven.* [11]*Blessed are ye, when men shall revile you, and persecute you, and shall say all manner of evil against you falsely, for my sake.* [12]*Rejoice, and be exceeding glad: for great is your reward in heaven: for so persecuted they the prophets which were before you*" (Matthew 5).

Countless books have been written on this portion of Scripture, generally referred to as the Beatitudes, but do we understand the core message? Is it that God promises to be with the underdog?

Picture yourself as a traveler on the road nearby. You hear Jesus speaking these words in a clear voice: *"Blessed are the poor in spirit: for theirs is the kingdom of heaven. Blessed are they that mourn for they shall be comforted..."* You are fascinated by these words, so you move closer and with the other bystanders sit at the feet of Jesus to listen to what He has to say. His disciples had just recently been called and they are sitting close to Him. It is His inaugural speech and I'm sure the listeners were fascinated by these words, but they could not really grasp the deeper meaning. It was a brilliant way to catch their attention and to make them curious as to what He was saying. What He was saying differed drastically from popular beliefs. The rich and proud were thought of as being blessed, but no, according to Luke 6, Jesus even added some woes describing them.

> "[24]But woe unto you that are rich! for ye have received your consolation. [25]Woe unto you that are full! for ye shall hunger. Woe unto you that laugh now! for ye shall mourn and weep. [26]Woe unto you, when all men shall speak well of you! for so did their fathers to the false prophets."

Yet, those who listened to Jesus were enthralled by his words which gave blessings and hope to those who least expected it. He promised hope to those who felt inadequate and in need of salvation.

The repetition of the words "blessed are" is followed by a category of afflicted people, followed by a promise. Seeing the picture as a whole one cannot assume that all people who are, for instance mourning because of the death of a loved one are blessed, but that the words: *"for my sake"* tells us that Jesus was referring to spiritual matters.

Studying this section in retrospect makes it clear that Jesus was describing the *character* of a true follower of Christ, especially when focusing on the *promises* that were attached to each of these attributes:

- theirs is the kingdom of heaven
- they shall be comforted
- they shall inherit the earth
- they shall be filled (with righteousness)
- they shall obtain mercy
- they shall see God
- they shall be called the children of God
- theirs is the kingdom of heaven (for the second time)
- great *is* your reward in heaven

The term "blessed" is often translated into English as "happy" which does not portray the whole picture. The meaning of the word "blessed" entails being happy because God cares for and loves you. Who can bless but God? So this "blessed" includes a happiness and peacefulness that comes from knowing that God is supporting you; that He is close to you and loves you.

Let's take a closer look at the characteristics of those belonging to the kingdom of heaven:

Poor in spirit: The many religious laws, traditions and rituals that the Pharisees added to the Law of God made most people feel utterly incompetent as far as spiritual matters were concerned. The opposite of poor in spirit would be "proud, arrogant, above others with regards to spiritual matters". Looking at the opposites of the terms here described might be a good way to understand the true meaning of each phrase –

TABLE 1   OPPOSITE MEANING OF WORDS

ATTRIBUTE	OPPOSITE
The poor in spirit	Spiritually arrogant, accomplished, knowledgeable, learned
They that mourn	Nonchalant, happy-go-lucky, blasé
The meek	Proud, self-seeking, assertive, self-justifying, self-sufficient
They which do hunger and thirst after righteousness	Chasing after material riches, worldly fame, self-righteous, lawless
The merciful	Non-caring, ruthless, revengeful, hateful, selfish
The pure in heart	Vulgar, deceitful, profane, blasphemous, incongruent, perverse
The peacemakers	Troublemakers, rebels, in enmity with God and his Law[7]
They which are persecuted	Popular, esteemed, famous
When *men* shall revile you, and persecute *you*, and shall say all manner of evil against you falsely,	Important, liked – especially for spreading a false doctrine, distinguished, popular in the world

---

[7] Ps. 119:165

In the light of what we get to know about the Pharisees, it is clear that the Pharisees could neatly fit into the picture describing the complete opposite of the people to whom Jesus promised the kingdom of heaven. This makes it easy to understand why He was so unpopular with this group from the start.

In the light of the above we can look again at the definition of those to whom the Kingdom of Heaven belongs, by using our Thesaurus:

TABLE 2 DEFINITION OF THOSE TO WHOM THE KINGDOM OF HEAVEN BELONGS

ATTRIBUTE	FURTHER MEANING
The poor in spirit	Humble, contrite, dependent on Jesus for salvation, broken
They that mourn	Sad, because of their awareness of their own incompetence, dire circumstances, sinfulness and also sorrowful on account of the wickedness of the world
The meek	Submissive to God and his Word, eager to listen and obey; not clever in own eyes, trusting Jesus in everything (like lambs following their Shepherd)[8], practicing self-control

---

[8] Joh.21:15

They which do hunger and thirst after righteousness	An eagerness to learn and do the will and law of God, to be saved; hope in the restoration of creation and of eternal life
The merciful	Compassionate, gracious, loving, forgiving, giving, serving others
The pure in heart	Genuine, true, cleansed, congruent/ pure motives, truthful, sincere, honest, upright
The peacemakers	Seeking calmness, sound relationships with others, peace, rest, love, truth and to be in harmony with God and his law.[9]
They which are persecuted	True to their faith and trust in Jesus/ willing to follow Jesus despite persecution or abandonment.
When *men* shall revile you and persecute *you*, and shall say all manner of evil against you falsely	When people badger, tease, mock, despise you, falsely accuse you for Jesus' sake, especially for speaking the truth about Him and His Word

If we study the section as a whole again it now becomes clearer how the first part of a Beatitude matches up with the second part or promise. It becomes clearer how this section should be

---

[9] Ps 119:165

understood in its entirety. In the following table the words in italics are added for a better understanding:

TABLE 3 CHARACTERISTIC AND PROMISE

CHARACTERISTIC	PROMISE THROUGH JESUS AS SAVIOUR
Blessed are the poor in spirit	theirs is the kingdom of heaven *(eternal life with God)*
[4]Blessed *are* they that mourn	they shall be comforted *(by Jesus)*
[5]Blessed *are* the meek	they shall inherit the earth *(the new earth)*
[6]Blessed *are* they which do hunger and thirst after righteousness	they shall be filled *(with righteousness imparted to them by Jesus Christ)*
[7]Blessed *are* the merciful	they shall obtain mercy *(forgiveness from Jesus)*
[8]Blessed *are* the pure in heart	they shall see God *(experience his presence in heaven)*
[9]Blessed *are* the peacemakers	they shall be called the children of God *(Christians – having a Christlike character)*
[10]Blessed *are* they which are persecuted for righteousness' sake:	theirs is the kingdom of heaven *(eternal life)*
[11]Blessed are ye, when *men* shall revile you, and persecute *you*, and shall say all manner of evil against you falsely, for my sake. [12]Rejoice, and be exceeding glad:	great *is* your reward in heaven: for so persecuted they the prophets which were before you.

It does not therefore really make sense to give someone a text such as: *"Blessed are they that mourn: for they shall be comforted"* on a sympathy card after they have lost a loved one, unless they understand the bigger picture. Yes, if you are a Christian, you could be able to grasp the meaning of the text, but only if you understand the bigger picture. If Jesus is the center of your life, you shall be comforted, if you allow Him to direct your life. You will be comforted in many ways:

- His Spirit will come close to you and give you peace and strength
- His salvation promises the hope of eternal life – taking away the fear of death

It becomes apparent that the rewards of those who follow Jesus will be for this present life (theirs is the kingdom of heaven), but also in the future (e.g. inherit the earth, see God). Those things which seem to be to our disadvantage in this life: e.g. humbling experiences, poverty and persecution for Jesus' sake, are just temporal set backs which we will overcome through faith in Jesus and the power of the Holy Spirit and we will be rewarded in eternity.[10]

Right from the start the followers of Jesus should have taken note of those things that were *not* promised:

---

[10] Isa.57:15

- Political freedom for the followers of Jesus – an earthly kingdom/ government or salvation by being part of any bigger group as a whole
- Material wealth and prosperity
- Fame or acceptance by the masses
- Care-free living conditions[11]

Yet, He did promise ultimate victory to those that overcome through providing for them comfort and strength.[12]

The order in which the beatitudes follow each other portrays Christian growth:

- being down-hearted, humble (poor in spirit) (Rev.3:17)
- being aware of own sin (mourn) (through the working of the Holy Spirit – John 16:8)
- being aware of own dependence (meek)
- being encouraged to listen to God's Word and accepting His plan of salvation, (hunger and thirst after righteousness) thus
- acting upon the prompting of his Spirit (merciful)
- demonstrating a change of character, obeying his law (for righteousness' sake) and experiencing true peace.[13] (pure in heart)
- being willing to be persecuted for Jesus (peacemakers)

---

[11] Matthew 10:34-38
[12] Rev.3:12; Joh.16:33
[13] Isa.55:13; Ps. 51:12

- that which makes no sense to the world – a broken spirit, dependency upon Jesus and the Holy Spirit, being persecuted in this world for our beliefs – will result in our exaltation to see God and be part of his heavenly kingdom forever. [14] (great is our reward in heaven)

To summarize, it can be said that this section does not contain direct instructions, but rather a description of the characteristics and conditions of those who belong to Jesus' kingdom of heaven. To his audience present at the time, the meaning of the words would only become clearer as time went by.

The next section also deals with the followers of Christ. This time it concentrates more on the mission of Christians – their influence upon the world.

> *"[13]Ye are the salt of the earth: but if the salt have lost his savour, wherewith shall it be salted? it is thenceforth good for nothing, but to be cast out, and to be trodden under foot of men. [14]Ye are the light of the world. A city that is set on an hill cannot be hid. [15]Neither do men light a candle, and put it under a bushel, but on a candlestick; and it giveth light unto all that are in the house. [16]Let your light so shine before men, that they may see your good works, and glorify your Father which is in heaven."*

Two symbols are used to illustrate the influence of (the way of being) Christians in the world: salt and light. It is remarkable how Jesus always used symbols that would be valid throughout the ages.

---

[14] Isa.61:3; Isa.57:18; Jer. 31:13

Salt preserves, purifies (disinfects), gives taste and supplies the body with essential minerals. In the same way the Christians should be preservers of the law and pure in character. Through the love and the power imparted by the Holy Spirit the message of salvation would give meaning to lives as salt gives savor to food. It is the mission of the followers of Jesus to let their influence permeate the world, similar to the above characteristic of salt.

Christians are not expected to isolate themselves from the world, but to have an effect on the people around them. They have an obligation to keep moral standards pure, by living every principle of the Word of God. They are essential to spread the truth of God throughout the world.

The salt used in Jesus' time were lumps taken from the inland lakes and used until it became soiled, when it was thrown out on the foot paths for people to trample on.

If you prepare soup with just the right amount of salt, it will be tasty, but if you keep adding water, it will lose its saltiness and become tasteless/ insipid. The same will happen to Christians who lose their identity, who dilute their characters with worldliness and thereby display a watered-down image of Christ.

Let's compare a newly converted Christian to whole-some tasty soup. How and why will he or she lose their taste?

We can take for granted that the devil hates no one more than a newly converted Christian. He will do his utmost best to put such a person on a false trail, or to crowd his or her thoughts with cares and troubles of this world. Jesus warned us about this in Luke 21:34: *"But take heed to yourselves, lest your hearts be weighed down with carousing, drunkenness, and cares of this life and that Day come upon you unexpectedly."* This is a warning about our involvement with worldly things at His Second Coming – more about this later.

Conforming to the world is not a problem of newly converted Christians only, but very much so for those who accepted the Lord as their Savior long ago. We are warned about this at several instances and by different Bible writers, e.g. James 4:4, 1 John 2:15-17. Divided loyalty is not accepted by God, as is stated in James 4:4:

"Do you not know that friendship with the world is enmity with God."

When we, the Christians, conform to the standards of the world our influence become diluted ending up being lukewarm – having no significant influence on the world around us (Rev.3:14-17).

The philosophy of this world is based on individualism, (psychology of self-worship) materialism, (never enough things) and entertainment (drown your thoughts with pleasant feelings) – be these of a sensual/ musical/ gourmet/ comical/ cinematic origin (2Tim.3:1-5).

Giving God first priority in our lives, in contrast to the pull of the world, becomes a daily battle for every Christian. (Gal.5:16-18; Gal.6:7,14; 1 John 2:15-17).

What will happen to those who give the world priority over God? They will eventually *be cast out*[15].

"Ye are the light of the world". Right from the start Jesus makes his followers aware of their global mission, of how they are to spread his truth. Light is a symbol of truth and of the only enlightening truth that can save a soul: namely redemption through Jesus Christ, our Savior. It eliminates darkness – the symbol of sin, ignorance and falsehood. The followers of Jesus are to be the light of the world as He is.

On the first day of creation God created light.[16] God is light, also in a literal sense. Wherever He was present, there was light, as was revealed in Moses' encounter with God on Mount Sinai.[17] In Revelation we read that in the New Jerusalem there will be no sun, for God will be our light.[18]

Jesus came to spread the light of the true character of God; to dispel the false image that the world had about the Father.

---

[15] Rev. 3:16
[16] Gen.1:3
[17] Ex.24:10,16,17
[18] Rev. 21:23

Satan is called the prince of darkness. From the beginning it was his mission to spread lies about the true character of God, to promote counterfeit religions and forms of worship. A good example is sun worship that existed from the earliest times. Instead of worshipping the true light, God, the people worshipped the sun – a creation of God.[19] The world today is applauding every false teaching that existed from the fall of man, and misconceptions of the Bible and the will of God. It is apparent that most people on earth today are bewildered, stressed and under impressions of the meaninglessness of life. When people cannot see due to darkness, they stumble and fall. Jesus is portrayed as a mystic being to which all kinds of misrepresentations are allotted.

In the Bible the movements of Jesus and many of the words He spoke were recorded. He had no material belongings except for the clothes on His back. The words He spoke were written down by four different authors. He was up-front and out-in-the-open. That which was recorded by the Gospel writers, was validated by the members of the first church, as many of those members were present at His gatherings (John 21:24, 25; Acts 4:10-12).

The followers of Jesus should be carriers of the light and be the opposite of darkness. The words: *"light of the world"* also emphasizes the global mission of

---

[19] Gen.1:16

Christians in spreading the gospel throughout the whole world, like taking torches into areas of darkness. (John 17:18)

The people listening to Jesus' sermon could envisage the villages surrounding them and how they were situated on the hills. They could identify with a lamp or candle on a candlestick to enable everyone to see. The light makes it possible for everyone to see around them, to grasp the bigger picture. With the phrase *"hiding under a bushel (bucket)"* Jesus emphasizes that his teachings are not to be inclusive – only for a chosen few – but to enlighten everyone with whom it comes into contact. We also know what will happen to a candle if you put a bucket over it. Hiding the light can also be interpreted as being scared or ashamed to openly proclaim God's truth. We should be compelled by Christ's love to share the gospel of salvation with others.

The character of a Christian should be a reflection of the greater Light in his life. The source of light is from within (Jesus Christ within us)[20] and so we testify to all around us. We are known to others through our words and deeds and through these we will encourage or discourage others to become Christians. A Christian should let his/her light shine like the sun which radiates light and warmth. In this

---

[20] Luke 17:21

manner the truth and love of Christ should radiate from the true Christian (1 John 2:8-10).

While the above section dealt with the way Christians should live to influence the world, and the Beatitudes painted the characteristics of the Christian, Jesus thereafter launched a full scale sermon on the interpretation of the law.

> *"17 Think not that I am come to destroy the law, or the prophets: I am not come to destroy, but to fulfil. 18For verily I say unto you, Till heaven and earth pass, one jot or one tittle shall in no wise pass from the law, till all be fulfilled. 19Whosoever therefore shall break one of these least commandments, and shall teach men so, he shall be called the least in the kingdom of heaven: but whosoever shall do and teach them, the same shall be called great in the kingdom of heaven. 20For I say unto you, That except your righteousness shall exceed the righteousness of the scribes and Pharisees, ye shall in no case enter into the kingdom of heaven."*

In no uncertain terms Jesus declared that the law and the prophets stand and that nothing was going to change it. He came to fulfill it. He would be an example of perfect obedience to the law. It becomes clear further on that He is referring to the Ten Commandments when He speaks about the law. Several prophets predicted the coming of the Messiah,[21] and it was thus clear that His coming was the fulfillment of these prophecies. As was mentioned earlier He often quoted from the law and the prophets. God's law would remain changeless and eternal.[22]

---

[21] Isa.7:14; Hosea 11:1, Micah 5:1,2

How did He come to fulfill the law? By living a life of perfect obedience to God and His will even unto death.[23] He did not come to destroy it and He declared that it is a commendable thing to teach and do the law. It is also wrong to teach others to disobey the law. To the people's amazement, however, He stated that their righteousness should exceed that of the scribes and Pharisees - something that must have shocked his audience. Everyone knew how inflexible the scribes and Pharisees were when it came to the interpretation of the law. Jesus was stating that to be like them was not good enough and that they *"shall in no case enter into the kingdom of heaven."* He showed them the true spirit of the law. "Righteousness" directly refers to obedience to the law of God.[24] The keeping of the law thus has implications for entering the kingdom of heaven. We are unable to keep the law out of our own strength and are therefore sinners condemned to die. Jesus would become our Sacrifice to work atonement for our sins.[25] If we love Him we will keep His commandments (1 John 5:1-3).

The scribes and Pharisees did not understand the principles of the law, and through their false interpretations made the law an unbearable burden to the people. They were unable to distinguish between their own legalistic misinterpretations and

---

[22] Luke 16:17
[23] Isa.53:4,5; Matt.26:2
[24] Deut.6:25, Ps 98:9; Ps.119:142-144,172
[25] Isa.53:10-12

the essence of the law – which is love for God and fellow men manifested in our words and deeds in practical every day living. Through His own obedience to the law Jesus demonstrated its basic truths. The law of God is a reflection of His holy character.[26] This is in contrast to the sinfulness of man.

Jesus continued and explained the principles underlying the Ten Commandments.

> "*21Ye have heard that it was said by them of old time, Thou shalt not kill; and whosoever shall kill shall be in danger of the judgment: 22But I say unto you, That whosoever is angry with his brother without a cause shall be in danger of the judgment: and whosoever shall say to his brother, Raca, shall be in danger of the council: but whosoever shall say, Thou fool, shall be in danger of hell fire. 23Therefore if thou bring thy gift to the altar, and there rememberest that thy brother hath ought against thee; 24Leave there thy gift before the altar, and go thy way; first be reconciled to thy brother, and then come and offer thy gift. 25Agree with thine adversary quickly, whiles thou art in the way with him; lest at any time the adversary deliver thee to the judge, and the judge deliver thee to the officer, and thou be cast into prison. 26Verily I say unto thee, Thou shalt by no means come out thence, till thou hast paid the uttermost farthing.*"

The crowd must have been spell bound. They had never had this kind of insight into the law (commandments) before. With the words: *"But I say unto you"* Jesus affirmed that He was an authority on the subject. Jesus said that it is not good enough to abstain from killing others. Even if you are angry at

---

[26] Ps.19:7,8

others without a cause you are committing a sin. In line with the knowledge of Jesus' attitude about forgiving seventy times seven (which is mentioned later in Matthew) one wonders if there could ever be a cause that would justify our anger. He also mentioned that it was more important to set our relationship right with someone before bringing a sacrifice. The idea is repeated later on: I want mercy more than sacrifice.[27] Also important here is to take note that it is your brother that has something against you and not the other way around, like we would expect. Christ emphasizes the obligation we have towards others. Being kind to your enemy was definitely not the way the Jews interpreted the law, as was evident in their hatred of the Romans and Samaritans at that time. It was probably also not a message they cared to hear at that time. Verse 26 has a ring of judgment again.

> "[27]Ye have heard that it was said by them of old time, Thou shalt not commit adultery: [28]But I say unto you, That whosoever looketh on a woman to lust after her hath committed adultery with her already in his heart. [29]And if thy right eye offend thee, pluck it out, and cast it from thee: for it is profitable for thee that one of thy members should perish, and not that thy whole body should be cast into hell. [30]And if thy right hand offend thee, cut it off, and cast it from thee: for it is profitable for thee that one of thy members should perish, and not that thy whole body should be cast into hell. [31] It hath been said, Whosoever shall put away his wife, let him give her a writing of divorcement: [32]But I say unto you, That whosoever shall put away his wife, saving for the cause of fornication, causeth her to commit

---

[27] Matt.12:7; Hosea 6:6

adultery: and whosoever shall marry her that is divorced committeth adultery."

Jesus shot directly at the hearts of people and also at the core of many problems. He used the example of men looking at women with lust in their eyes. His solution to the problems might sound pretty harsh to us. Jesus used a hyperbole/exaggeration to illustrate the seriousness of the matter to His audience. Our physical body could rather perish than us losing eternal life. Sin finds an entry point through our senses. Evil thoughts should be withstood immediately. Our physical bodies are to die eventually, but our transformed bodies are to inherit the eternal kingdom of heaven.[28] By using this example of the plucking out of the eye, He was trying to get his audience to grasp the truth that spiritual well-being has priority over physical well-being. He would teach this idea again later.[29]

In no uncertain terms, Jesus spelled out that divorce, except in the case of illicit sexual relationships, equals adultery which was forbidden by the law. Divorce equals sin which is the transgression of the law of God. It is not an unpardonable sin, as some would make it out to be. Jesus would discuss the unpardonable sin later on. Looking at a woman with lust on your mind is also adultery, in other words, sin, according to Jesus.

---

[28] 1Thes.4:16,17
[29] Matt.15:17-20

Jesus died for us so that we can be cleansed of our sins. All we have to do is to confess our sins and accept His gift of salvation (1 John 1:7-9).

> "[33]Again, ye have heard that it hath been said by them of old time, Thou shalt not forswear thyself, but shalt perform unto the Lord thine oaths: [34]But I say unto you, Swear not at all; neither by heaven; for it is God's throne: [35]Nor by the earth; for it is his footstool: neither by Jerusalem; for it is the city of the great King. [36]Neither shalt thou swear by thy head, because thou canst not make one hair white or black. [37]But let your communication be, Yea, yea; Nay, nay: for whatsoever is more than these cometh of evil."

A clear and distinct instruction: do not swear, that is a solemn statement to confirm the truth. What was implied here was perjury in which the Jews often partook – swearing by the temple, the gold of the temple, the altar etc. These customs are also later discussed in Matthew 23:16-22. Perjury that invokes the name of God and thereby dishonors or profanes his name, is sin[30]

We should seriously consider oaths that we have made to God – *"shalt perform unto the Lord thine oaths"*. The seriousness of such oaths was described in the Old Testament.[31]

The words we speak should be truthful and transparent. If people trust and respect us, they know that our yes means yes and our no means no.

---

[30] Lev.19:12
[31] Num 30:2; Deut.23:21

> "*³⁸Ye have heard that it hath been said, An eye for an eye, and a tooth for a tooth: ³⁹But I say unto you, That ye resist not evil: but whosoever shall smite thee on thy right cheek, turn to him the other also. ⁴⁰And if any man will sue thee at the law, and take away thy coat, let him have thy cloak also. ⁴¹And whosoever shall compel thee to go a mile, go with him twain. ⁴²Give to him that asketh thee, and from him that would borrow of thee turn not thou away.*"

This is a very hard instruction and it goes against our human nature. Children demonstrate the notion of human nature so plainly. He hit me, so I hit him back. But Jesus says, no, we must do the unexpected: turn the other cheek, give to him that sues you – even more than he wanted, go the extra mile, lend to him that wants to borrow from you. Again the emphasis is on the importance of human relationships, on humility and submission. We are not to assume the role of judging. We should let go of our self-centeredness and our self-righteousness. Jesus emphasized that human relationships are more important than material gain.

> "*⁴³Ye have heard that it hath been said, Thou shalt love thy neighbour, and hate thine enemy. ⁴⁴But I say unto you, Love your enemies, bless them that curse you, do good to them that hate you, and pray for them which despitefully use you, and persecute you; ⁴⁵That ye may be the children of your Father which is in heaven: for he maketh his sun to rise on the evil and on the good, and sendeth rain on the just and on the unjust. ⁴⁶For if ye love them which love you, what reward have ye? do not even the publicans the same? ⁴⁷And if ye salute your brethren only, what do ye more than others? do not*

even the publicans so? ⁴⁸Be ye therefore perfect, even as your Father which is in heaven is perfect."

Wow! Now Jesus seems to be taking things just too far. Love your enemy? It has been said that many of the things that Jesus taught, were also taught by other prophets, even amongst other religions, but that this specific instruction was something that distinguished Him from the others. Is this humanly impossible? Yes, probably if we try to do this in our own strength, but if we ask Him He will give us the power to carry out this instruction. He will send the Holy Spirit to assist us to overcome evil (Luke 11:13; John 16:13,14).

The definition of love (agapao) that Jesus refers to includes respect and courtesy and is not based on emotions alone. It encompasses the mind and a cognitive choice. We are commanded to treat our enemies courteously and with respect. We are expected to be kind to our enemies to diffuse their anger against us. Jesus even gives us practical examples of how to do this: bless them, do good to them, pray for them.

Because of the existence of sin in the world, it seems as if Jesus accepted the fact that we will always have enemies, often not of our own doing. When we do what is right we will be hated by those whose conscience accuses them.[32] It is in our own interest not to hate.[33] Jesus considers hatred in the

---

[32] Joh.15:18,19,23

same sense as murder, according to Matthew 5:21 & 22.

God maintains the earth and everybody on it – whether they are good or evil. Who are we to make distinctions and treat some people with less respect than others?

Then the instruction follows that sounds just as impossible to achieve: be ye perfect (flawless/complete). But later on we will understand: we can be perfect if we are perfectly dependent on Jesus. Christ wants us to reflect his character. He wants us to see the essence of the law: to lift our aims to the high ideals of God's love and his intention for us to love one another – to put the other's needs above our own. Our inner motives and attitudes will determine our actions and contribute to our formation of character. God sees our hearts. The law will judge our acts. If we love God and our fellow human beings the way we should, thoughts to break the law should not even cross our minds.

From this section comes a few underlying themes:

- the importance of the law and the prophets; Jesus came to fulfill (implement/ carry out/ execute/ complete) the law and prophets;
- the flesh versus the spirit with the greater importance of the latter;

---

[33] Eccles.12:14; Matt.22:36-40

- the great importance of our relationship with other human beings, be they on a friendly foot with us or not;
- the deeper meaning and right interpretation of the law of God;
- the aim to have a perfect, Christlike character and through the power of the Holy Spirit overcome our dislike for our adversaries.

In viewing this section as a whole, it is clear that this was a deliberate attempt by Jesus to clarify the people's misunderstanding of the law of God. The bad behavior resulting in the transgression of the law, has its origin in the mind of man. A person should guard against even thinking wrong thoughts before these thoughts result in bad behavior. Jesus intensified the keeping of the law by emphasizing the fact that bad behavior has it's origin in our minds.

> "[1]Take heed that ye do not your alms before men, to be seen of them: otherwise ye have no reward of your Father which is in heaven. [2]Therefore when thou doest thine alms, do not sound a trumpet before thee, as the hypocrites do in the synagogues and in the streets, that they may have glory of men. Verily I say unto you, They have their reward. [3]But when thou doest alms, let not thy left hand know what thy right hand doeth: [4]That thine alms may be in secret: and thy Father which seeth in secret himself shall reward thee openly" (Matthew 6).

Again Jesus focused on our motives. We should be good to others, but not for the purpose to be seen and praised by them. This was the typical conduct of the Pharisees. If the Pharisees were a political party, Jesus would have been the leader of the opposition party, as He goes out of his way to teach the direct opposite of what they were doing. Many wealthy people thrive on the acknowledgement given to them by the charities they support. Some make such a show of the gifts they bestow on others – no wonder Jesus said that they have had their reward.

Some of our acts should be done in private (in secret): acts of charity and fasting (Matthew 6:4, 6 & 18). These are between you and God. The phrase *"let not thy left hand know what thy right hand doeth"*, implies that our acts of charity should just happen naturally without us making an issue of it – whether through outward appearances or in our own minds. The Christian's life should be characterized by acts of unselfishness, without putting on a show. God will ultimately repay his followers for their acts of kindness.[34]

> *"⁵And when thou prayest, thou shalt not be as the hypocrites are: for they love to pray standing in the synagogues and in the corners of the streets, that they may be seen of men. Verily I say unto you, They have their reward. ⁶But thou, when thou prayest, enter into thy closet, and when thou hast shut thy door, pray to thy Father which is in secret; and thy Father which seeth in secret shall reward thee openly. ⁷But when ye pray, use not vain repetitions, as the heathen do: for they think that they shall be heard for their much speaking.*

---

[34] Matt. 25:34

> *⁸Be not ye therefore like unto them: for your Father knoweth what things ye have need of, before ye ask him."*

Again Jesus steered his followers away from the way the Pharisees were behaving. He counsels us to pray in private. He gave an example of what such a prayer should contain in Matthew 6:9-13. It is clear that Jesus emphasized true and sincere worship which was in direct contrast to hypocritical shows of piety meant to impress others.

> *"⁹After this manner therefore pray ye: Our Father which art in heaven, Hallowed be Thy name. ¹⁰Thy kingdom come. Thy will be done in earth, as it is in heaven. ¹¹Give us this day our daily bread. ¹²And forgive us our debts, as we forgive our debtors. ¹³And lead us not into temptation, but deliver us from evil: For Thine is the kingdom, and the power, and the glory, for ever. Amen. ¹⁴For if ye forgive men their trespasses, your heavenly Father will also forgive you: ¹⁵But if ye forgive not men their trespasses, neither will your Father forgive your trespasses."*

In our modern times we want to shun away from the way Jesus started his prayer: through worship and adoration – exalting the name of the Father:

> *"Our Father which art in heaven, Hallowed be Thy name. ¹⁰Thy kingdom come. Thy will be done in earth, as it is in heaven."*

It is important how we address God in the introduction of our prayer. We should acknowledge our position and that of our Father. We are children of the Father – what a wonderful position, greater than any words can describe![35] This demonstrates

His love for us. There is the further implication that we have brothers and sisters in Christ whom we should also love and be grateful for. As close family of God we should take a keen interest in His will, His honor, His character, His law and His word.

We want His kingdom to come and His will to be done on earth as is the case in heaven. This implies that although the coming of Jesus to this earth for the first time was announced as the kingdom being at hand, the fulfillment of that momentous occasion lies in the future.[36] This will be when Jesus comes again to reign as King of kings. Through these words we acknowledge that all power and glory belong to God and that we want Him to come soon and take full control of the earth. Jesus implied that God's will is done in heaven, which also indicates that our earth is the only fallen world.

Then followed the supplications:

> "[11]Give us this day our daily bread. [12]And forgive us our debts, as we forgive our debtors. [13]And lead us not into temptation, but deliver us from evil."

Only after honoring the name of God, do we come with our petitions. Before adding our own list of requests, it is essential that God grants us these basics every day: daily bread (declaring our physical dependence as well as our spiritual dependence), forgiveness (declaring our need for

---

[35] John 1:12
[36] Matthew 25:31-34

the cleansing of our mind), and protection from evil (declaring our utter dependence on God, being unable to stand against the evil forces in our own strength). Jesus emphasized the fact that we should live one day at a time. Days are bite-size portions of living. We need to ask for the things we need on a daily basis, thus encouraging us to communicate often with God and declare our dependence on Him.[37] Jesus would explain that He is to be our living bread, satisfying our spiritual hunger.[38]

Jesus would pay the penalty for our sins so that we could be truly forgiven. Out of love and gratitude towards Him, we should be forgiving toward those who wronged us. On this condition only can we claim forgiveness. This was also illustrated to us by Jesus through the parable in Matthew 18:23-35.

Temptations come from Satan and from our own sinful and selfish inclinations. If we can stand fast in our faith in Jesus when temptations come, our characters will grow stronger. We know that the devil wants to destroy us, but that God will ultimately destroy him and his evil angels.[39] As long as we depend on Jesus Christ, the Father and the Holy Spirit, evil cannot prevail.[40]

The prayer is ended by again giving praise to God: *"For Thine is the kingdom, and the power, and the glory, for ever".* The

---

[37] Luke 11:9-13
[38] Joh.6:35,48,51
[39] Rev.20:10
[40] Eph.6:18,23,24; James 4:7

fact that God is the only God worthy of worship was again emphasized.

From the *Lord's Prayer*, as it is commonly known, we learn a few interesting facts:

- God is in heaven and He is *our* Holy Father – we want His name to be uplifted as holy – that specific characteristic that only He possesses.
- The kingdom of heaven is at hand. This message was preached by John the Baptist, Jesus and His disciples as they started their ministries.[41] We are looking forward to the conclusion when He comes on the clouds of heaven to judge the world.
- God's will is done in heaven.
- We are totally dependent on God for our physical well-being, for our daily sustenance, for the forgiveness of our sins and for protection against the schemes of the evil one. And we should acknowledge this and ask for these things on a daily basis.
- God is the only God who has power and glory forever.
- Jesus emphasizes the importance to us of forgiving those who sin against us. We should do unto others as we wish to be treated ourselves.[42]

> "*[16]Moreover when ye fast, be not, as the hypocrites, of a sad countenance: for they disfigure their faces, that they may appear unto men to fast. Verily I say unto you, They have their reward. [17]But thou, when thou fastest, anoint thine head, and wash thy face; [18]That thou appear not unto men to fast, but unto thy Father which is in secret: and thy Father, which seeth in secret, shall reward thee openly.*"

---

[41] Matthew 3:2, and 10:7
[42] Matt.7:12

Jesus was affirming that fasting is good. The way we should do it should again not resemble the way the Pharisees fasted. Here again, Jesus states in no uncertain terms that we should not be like hypocrites, trying to impress others by our religious piety. Fasting should be accompanied by a contrite heart and an earnest seeking of the will of God. It is the pursuing of a personal experience with God. Long faces do not portray genuine religion.

> *"[19]Lay not up for yourselves treasures upon earth, where moth and rust doth corrupt, and where thieves break through and steal: [20]But lay up for yourselves treasures in heaven, where neither moth nor rust doth corrupt, and where thieves do not break through nor steal: [21]For where your treasure is, there will your heart be also."*

We tend to accumulate a lot of worldly goods to give ourselves a false feeling of security. We think it will help us to cope with our fears for the future. The truth is that all these things deteriorate: moth and rust are constantly at work. All material things are prone to age, it will depreciate and "wither" away. Even strong buildings can crumble through earthquakes or wars. Instead of giving us security these things make us anxious when thieves break in and steal. Jesus set the example of what He meant by owning nothing, except the clothes on his back. We should accumulate treasures in heaven. Surely this statement should have made his audience curious about what these treasures are, and how they are to be accumulated. His further teachings would shed more light on the subject.

Where your treasure is, there your heart will also be. This is so true of us humans. Our thoughts and motives spill over in our words and deeds. It becomes clear to all around us what our main concerns in life are. The love for money is still the strongest passion, enthused by selfish greed in the world today.[43] If we seek security in our possessions and financial provision for the future, we tend to see ourselves as self-sufficient and independent from God. We also tend to think that financial freedom will bring us ultimate happiness – hence the popularity of national lotteries and competitions. Yet there are numerous examples available to us of how this is not the case. More important issues are at stake with eternal value.[44] We are advised by Jesus to *"lay up treasures in heaven"*.[45]

> *"22The light of the body is the eye: if therefore thine eye be single, thy whole body shall be full of light. 23But if thine eye be evil, thy whole body shall be full of darkness. If therefore the light that is in thee be darkness, how great is that darkness."*

This section has its parallel in Luke 11:34-36:

> *"34The light of the body is the eye: therefore when thine eye is single, thy whole body also is full of light; but when thine eye is evil, thy body also is full of darkness. 35Take heed therefore that the light which is in thee be not darkness. 36If thy whole body therefore be full of light, having no part dark, the whole shall be full of light, as when the bright shining of a candle doth give thee light."*

---

[43] 1 Tim.6:10; Hebr.13:5
[44] Luke 21:34-36
[45] Math.13:44

Often in the Old[46] as well as in the New Testament[47] the symbol of the eye is used to demonstrate wisdom, insight and understanding. Making use of this striking symbol, which would always be part of our humanness, Jesus again touches on our inner motives, spilling over into our behavior. A person can also be driven by something which he thinks is light, but in fact, is darkness. This comes out in the section in Luke:

> "*35Take heed therefore that the light which is in thee be not darkness.*"

This could also be seen to refer to false doctrines which many people would also enthusiastically believe to be the truth, but are indeed error.

The phrase *"thine eye is single"* could be translated as that your eye(mind) is sound/in a healthy condition. Our focus should be clear and honest and our commitment unadulterated.

If we live in darkness continuously, we will lose the ability to see.[48] It was especially hard for Jesus during His earthly mission, that people found it so hard to grasp the truth.[49] He healed many from physical blindness, but it was their spiritual blindness that made Him weep.[50]

---

[46] 2 Kings 6:17; Ps 13:3; Ps 119:18; Prov.4:25
[47] Luke 10:23; Hebr.11:27, Eph. 1:18
[48] 1 Joh.2:11
[49] Luke 19:42; Mark 8:18
[50] Matt.13:14,15

The theme of light versus darkness is often used as symbols in the controversy between God and Satan, good and evil (see table 4).

Jesus stated it as a fact that no man *can* serve two masters. The principles of the kingdom of heaven are totally different from that of this world. They are in fact, direct opposites as was just illustrated with the symbols of light and darkness. It is therefore imperative that a person must make up his mind to which system he belongs, and pledge his loyalty accordingly.

TABLE 4   LIGHT VERSUS DARKNESS

Light	Darkness
God,[51] Father, Jesus Christ, Holy Spirit	Satan and his evil angels[52]
The presence of God[53]	The animosity of Satan[54]
Truth[55]	Lies, apostasy [56]
Law of God[57]	Lawlessness[58]

---

[51] 1Joh.1:5; Joh.12:35,36; Joh.8:12
[52] Acts 26:18
[53] Ps 36:9; Job 22:28
[54] Eph.6:11,12
[55] Prov.20:27; Ps 43:3
[56] Rom.1:20,21,25; Rom.11:8-10; 1 Cor.4:5
[57] Prov.6:23; Ps.37:5,6
[58] 1 Sam.2:9; Acts 5:3;
[59] 1 Joh.2:9; 10
[60] 1 Joh.2:11
[61] 1 Joh.1:5-7; 1 Thes.5:5-8
[62] Rom.13:12,13; Eph.5:8,11
[63] 1 Joh.1:7
[64] Ps.119:105

Love[59]	Hatred[60]
Good deeds[61]	Evil deeds[62]
True worship[63] and the Word of God[64]	False religion[65]
Eternal life	Eternal death[66]

"24No man can serve two masters: for either he will hate the one, and love the other; or else he will hold to the one, and despise the other. Ye cannot serve God and mammon."

Someone who tries to serve God but at the same time loves the world, will be unstable and not trustworthy.[67] Those who serve mammon (earthly wealth) will be furthering its cause.[68]

"25Therefore I say unto you, Take no thought for your life, what ye shall eat, or what ye shall drink; nor yet for your body, what ye shall put on. Is not the life more than meat, and the body than raiment? 26Behold the fowls of the air: for they sow not, neither do they reap, nor gather into barns; yet your heavenly Father feedeth them. Are ye not much better than they? 27 Which of you by taking thought can add one cubit unto his stature? 28And why take ye thought for raiment? Consider the lilies of the field, how they grow; they toil not, neither do they spin: 29And yet I say unto you, That even Solomon in all his glory was not arrayed like one of these. 30Wherefore, if God so clothe the grass of the field, which today is, and tomorrow is cast into the oven, shall he not much more clothe you, O ye of little faith? 31Therefore take no thought, saying, What shall we eat? or, What shall we drink? or, Wherewithal shall we be clothed? 32(For after all these things do the Gentiles seek:) for your heavenly Father knoweth that ye have need of all these things. 33But seek ye first the kingdom

---

[65] 1 Joh.1:6
[66] Ps 49:18-20, Jude 1:5,6; 2 Pet.2:4
[67] James 4:4
[68] Rom.6:12-16

> of God, and His righteousness; and all these things shall be added unto you. ³⁴Take therefore no thought for the morrow: for the morrow shall take thought for the things of itself. Sufficient unto the day is the evil thereof."

At face value one might think that the message or principle that Jesus was teaching here is that of: "Don't worry, be happy" - to put it bluntly.

Yet, one of the main themes that Jesus was trying to get across, in fact in the following verse, was that our emphasis in life should be on spiritual matters more than on material matters.

> "³³But seek ye first the kingdom of God, and his righteousness; and all these things shall be added unto you."

He was also trying to get across the idea that we should learn to depend on God on a daily basis for our everyday needs. These include material as well as spiritual needs. He Himself is to be our Bread and Water. The idea is confirmed by the way Jesus Himself lived and depended on His Father. We learn from the Gospels that He spent a lot of time in prayer and meditation, and that He knew Scripture.[69]

To the serious Bible student a portion of Scripture like this poses endless possibilities to move to deeper levels of understanding through prayer and meditation and by using cross references with other sections in the Bible. For instance, there is the challenge to trust God in everything, such as the

---

[69] Matt.4:4,7,10

provision of food, clothing and health. Then there is the concept of the kingdom of God and His righteousness. It is clear that Jesus stressed the idea of prioritization, of grasping the important fact that spiritual issues are more important than everyday life issues.[70]

Another level of understanding would be a conscious decision to obey the words of Jesus. Only when we internalize the principles taught by Jesus on a personal level, will they become meaningful to us. If we are prepared to be truly honest and open to receive the guidance of His Holy Spirit, it will be possible for us to live out these principles.[71] But we cannot fight the inclination towards evil within ourselves by ourselves. We are often ignorant to the fact that our strength to live these principles also comes from God – we only have to ask for it. [72]

And yes, the instructions of Jesus are meant to be followed, to be obeyed.[73] They are not to be seen as soothing greeting card words – just to read and forget. That is why the title of this book is "The Commandments of Jesus Christ" – according to the words in Matthew 28:20 *"everything that I have commanded you."* It is meant as a wake-up call for Christians.

---

[70] Luke 21:34-36
[71] John 14:13-16,21; John 15:10-14
[72] Matthew 7:7,8
[73] Joh.15:14

To summarize, the following conclusions can be made regarding verses 25 to 34:

- Do not worry, or be overly concerned regarding material things and your own sustenance – God is in control, trust Him.
- Life is more than food and clothing. Our concerns should rather be with regard to spiritual things.
- The Father cares for the birds and plants, why would He neglect us – the crown of His creation?
- Worrying indicates that we do not have faith in our heavenly Father.
- What we should be seeking in all earnestness is the kingdom of God and His righteousness.[74]
- We should live and care about today and not tomorrow.

In view of Matt.6: 11-13 we should ask what we need from God and trust Him on a daily basis.

Matthew 7
"¹Judge not, that ye be not judged. ²For with what judgment ye judge, ye shall be judged: and with what measure ye mete, it shall be measured to you again. ³And why beholdest thou the mote that is in thy brother's eye, but considerest not the beam that is in thine own eye? ⁴Or how wilt thou say to thy brother, Let me pull out the mote out of thine eye; and, behold, a beam is in thine own eye? ⁵Thou hypocrite, first cast out the beam out of thine own eye; and then shalt thou see clearly to cast out the mote out of thy brother's eye."

Again, Jesus shot directly at the heart of one of our human weaknesses. Because of our own feelings of inferiority, we tend to think that it will make us feel better when we break others down. This condition

---

[74] Deut.6:25, Ps.119:172

usually has its roots in our own futile efforts to obey the law of God, while depending on our own strengths. Once we take our eyes off Jesus and become self-centered, we start the game of judging others. Where they fall short, we score points. Or so we reason. Have you ever said to your child: "The mark you got for maths is not good enough" upon which he immediately responded: "You should see Sammy's marks" or "The whole class did bad."

We are all on different levels of spiritual growth. When we criticize others, we can be certain that we have not progressed far. Some people are eager to bring about reform in others. Yet we all have room for improvement as Jesus said to the Pharisees later on:

> "He that is without sin among you, let him first cast a stone..." (John 8:7).

If we judge others, we create a standard, to which we ourselves seldom comply.[75] Only God can know a person's inner motives.[76]

It is a greater sin to have an unforgiving, insensitive and faultfinding attitude than whatever the defect (splinter) was that we so precariously tried to correct in another. Only Jesus Christ has the right to judge.[77] According to the example Jesus set on earth, we should draw others to Him by loving them.

---

[75] Rom.2:1
[76] 1 Cor.4:5
[77] Joh.5:22

That is our mission. He will be the ultimate Judge of all that was done and of everyone that ever lived.[78]

Again Jesus used the word "hypocrite" to describe the critical person, whose own motives are suspect, more willing to emphasize the mistakes of others than having a genuine concern for their well-being.

One injustice invokes another. With the measure we mete out to others, to that same extent we will be measured.[79]

> "*6Give not that which is holy unto the dogs, neither cast ye pearls before swine, lest they trample them under their feet, and turn again and rend you*".

Jesus now painted the other side of the coin: do not associate with those who clearly have no desire to depart from their erroneous thinking and those who ridicule the Gospel. In essence the word "holy" means consecrated to the service of the Lord.[80] If people do not respect or regard the things pertaining to the Lord, we should not waste our time with them. They should not be given the opportunity to ridicule the Gospel. Dogs and swine were regarded as unclean animals.

> "*7Ask, and it shall be given you; seek, and ye shall find; knock, and it shall be opened unto you: 8For every one that asketh receiveth; and he that seeketh findeth; and to him that knocketh it shall be opened. 9Or what man is there of you, whom if his son ask bread, will he give*

---

[78] Gen.18:25; Ps.94:1,2; Ps.7:11; Heb.12:22-24; 2Tim.4:8, Acts 10:42
[79] Mark 4:24; Luke 6:37,38
[80] Ex.40:9

him a stone? ¹⁰Or if he ask a fish, will he give him a serpent? ¹¹If ye then, being evil, know how to give good gifts unto your children, how much more shall your Father which is in heaven give good things to them that ask him?"

We are encouraged to ask, to take our concerns to the Lord. Again Jesus solicited us to submit to Him instead of trying to cope, depending on our own strengths. It is pride that keeps us from asking. We want to take care of ourselves. We strive to be independent. The whole world screams: You can do it. You are great. Believe in yourself. If you can dream it, you can do it. This is the message that is preached from the hilltops – and particularly on TV, in magazines, films and best-selling books. No need for any help from God – you are great on your own. Their philosophy seems to be: yes, do use God or church to achieve your goal if necessary. And it is possibly true that certain individuals achieve great heights, but these usually do not include a pure and spotless character, or obeying God's law of love. Jesus emphasized that worldly success or wealth is not the ultimate goal to be achieved, as He sets different standards.[81]

We need God and we need Him daily. We need Him for everything in our lives. If He does not grant us good health and peaceful surroundings, our ambitions will amount to absolutely nothing. We can save ourselves endless worries if we submit to

---

[81] Matt.6:33

Jesus Christ and depend on Him for everything in our lives. He gave us the assurance that He will respond. In the Lord's Prayer in Matthew 6 He showed us certain things that we should be asking for on a daily basis (bread, forgiveness and protection against evil).

The example of a child asking his father for bread, illustrated the way in which we should come to the Father with our earnest requests for the good things that we need: forgiveness, sustenance, health, love, peace, rest. We are God's children. He is a good Father and He will never forsake us.[82] The symbol of bread indicated that we should request that which is necessary to sustain us. Nowhere did Jesus ever preach the idea that his followers should claim a life of comfort and luxury.

> *"12Therefore all things whatsoever ye would that men should do to you, do ye even so to them: for this is the law and the prophets".*

This sentence is what is generally known as "The Golden Rule". What marvelous insight Jesus showed into human behavior. We ourselves set the norm: we expect others to behave in a certain way, to treat us with dignity and respect. We should do likewise. Put yourself in the other person's shoes. How would you react if you had to live under his conditions? This is commonly known as empathy. If your circumstances were different, you could be the

---

[82] Isa.49:14-16

person with disabilities, the prisoner, the poor or the aged. What would you do if you were in that situation? How would you expect others to behave towards you?

If you expect others to be honest, courteous, sensitive and caring, why don't you try these principles in your relationship with everyone you come across? If we put the needs of others before our own, our characters will be purified, our hearts softened. We expect others to care for us when we are broken-hearted, seriously ill or totally bankrupt. Therefore we should care for others in similar circumstances. The Golden Rule becomes the rule for the Christian life. Those who cannot identify with this principle, dare not call themselves Christians. Such was the example of the first Christians who shared everything.[83] The love and grace of Jesus should fill us with gratitude, and inspire us to give and to share.

The way in which we treat our fellow human beings will be the test of our sincerity and of our faith in Jesus Christ. This attitude of ours towards others reflects our relationship with God.[84]

He summarized: *"this is the law and the prophets"* (verses 7, 12). In other words: the essence of the law and message of the prophets are summed up in this simple fact to live by. The last six of the Ten

---

[83] Acts 4:32-34; Acts 2: 46,47
[84] 1 John 3:14-18

Commandments also deals with our relationship with other people. Jesus intensified these commandments by emphasizing that even the thoughts to treat others badly, are sinful. Treat others the way you would like to be treated yourself.

Another fact of life illustrated here, was that if we are friendly towards others, they will react accordingly and vice versa: if we treat them with hostility, they will react in a hostile way. Underlying this principle is the fact that we should love (respect/care for) ourselves. We have intrinsic value as children of God. If we are barred from this insight through sin, pride or guilt, we should come to God through the atoning blood of Jesus Christ and be cleansed.[85]

> "[13]Enter ye in at the strait gate: for wide is the gate, and broad is the way, that leadeth to destruction, and many there be which go in thereat: [14]Because strait is the gate, and narrow is the way, which leadeth unto life, and few there be that find it".

Our natural tendency is to "go with the flow". As the saying goes, "To follow the path of least resistance is what makes rivers and people crooked". With the least effort we can join in with those on the broad way.

It is to find the truth and live in obedience to the Word of God that takes careful consideration. Our daily choices have to be taken into account. We

---

[85] Eph.2:8

have to learn to say "No", "no thank you", or even "over my dead body" to many suggestions that come our way. For those who choose the narrow way the struggle is temporal, but the reward eternal. For those on the broad way the enjoyment is temporal, but the result is eternal destruction (death).[86] The rewards of both sides are temporal and eternal. Unfortunately for those on the broad way: they also experience disappointment, grief and pain. They fail to see the meaning of life and forego the presence and power of God to sustain them, and give them strength to overcome difficult situations. They often reap what they sow.

Being on the narrow way would mean that you are part of a minority group, since there are few that find it. Jesus says in John 14:6:

> "I am the way, the truth, and the life: no man cometh unto the Father, but by me".
> "[15]Beware of false prophets, which come to you in sheep's clothing, but inwardly they are ravening wolves. [16]Ye shall know them by their fruits. Do men gather grapes of thorns, or figs of thistles? [17]Even so every good tree bringeth forth good fruit; but a corrupt tree bringeth forth evil fruit. [18]A good tree cannot bring forth evil fruit, neither can a corrupt tree bring forth good fruit. [19]Every tree that bringeth not forth good fruit is hewn down, and cast into the fire. [20]Wherefore by their fruits ye shall know them."

By being mislead many who believe themselves to be on the narrow way, are actually heading for destruction by being deceived. Jesus warned on

---

[86] Rom.1:28-32; Rom.6:23; Gal.5:19-21

many occasions against false prophets and false doctrines.[87] Jesus knew beforehand that Satan would use "clever" people to hide the truth as clearly spoken by Him.

Thousands of books have been written on who Jesus really was, on the historical facts surrounding Him and the ways He should be interpreted, while His words were spoken with clarity and His core teachings repeated in the four Gospels to avoid misunderstandings. But do people listen and accept His instructions? No. The teachings of Jesus that do not suit their lifestyle must be rationalized away.[88]

Jesus advised us to look at the fruits of those who claim to proclaim His truths – in other words, what are the results, or works that follow their beliefs? The fruit to be expected of a converted Christian is unconditional obedience to His Law, manifesting as love, joy, peace, patience, kindness, goodness and faithfulness.[89]

Success as measured by the secular world is seen as owning big houses, flashy cars, designer clothes, large bank accounts, etc. Attempts to teach children to be honest and trustworthy without their hearts being changed by God's love, is of no avail. They will rather follow example than mere words.

---

[87] Matt.24:23,24
[88] 2 Tim.3:1-5
[89] Gal.5:22-25

"²¹Not every one that saith unto me, Lord, Lord, shall enter into the kingdom of heaven; but he that doeth the will of my Father which is in heaven. ²²Many will say to me in that day, Lord, Lord, have we not prophesied in thy name? and in thy name have cast out devils? and in thy name done many wonderful works? ²³And then will I profess unto them, I never knew you: depart from me, ye that work iniquity. ²⁴Therefore whosoever heareth these sayings of mine, and doeth them, I will liken him unto a wise man, which built his house upon a rock: ²⁵And the rain descended, and the floods came, and the winds blew, and beat upon that house; and it fell not: for it was founded upon a rock. ²⁶And every one that heareth these sayings of mine, and doeth them not, shall be likened unto a foolish man, which built his house upon the sand: ²⁷And the rain descended, and the floods came, and the winds blew, and beat upon that house; and it fell: and great was the fall of it."

A warning was given by Jesus that many people are going to be very unpleasantly surprised when they expect to be saved and have a place in heaven. Jesus is saying that many are quick to call Him Lord Lord, but they do not obey Him. They are still following Christ on their own terms and not His. They would be under the impression that they were spiritual leaders in the Christian church of their time due to the fact that they prophesied, cast out devils and had done miracles in the name of Jesus. To their utter amazement Jesus would answer them that He never knew them. It will be a great shock to them to hear that they *"worked iniquity"*. What does that mean? Jesus used the demonstration of two men who built houses – one on rock and the other on sand. The one that heard His Word without obeying is the one that built his house on sand. That one could not remain standing when the testing time came. It was not built on truth and therefore did not bear the right fruits.

Jesus had already explained that He did not come to do away with the Law (Ten Commandments) but to fulfill them. Those who work iniquity (lawlessness) are those who do not obey the Law and also teach others to do so. Everybody's works will be laid bare when judgment comes (Matt.13:41).

To summarize this section:

Many will know the name of the Lord and be under the impression that He knows them: but do they know Him? Are they preoccupied with their own good works or do they have a saving relationship with Christ? They will be active church members, yet they **do not do that which He told them to do** and give their lives over to Him; many will practice religion and fake conversion to impress others, but God knows everyone's deepest secrets and hidden motives;[90] but because people do not do the will of His Father – that is obey His Commandments - He does not acknowledge them; to their own defense they will actually mention the great works of religion they were involved in. He will not be impressed, and declares that He never knew them. He compares them to a house built on sand, washed away in the

---

[90] Matt.10:26

storm, because it had no foundation – Jesus Christ is our foundation.

People show that they do **not** love God by **not** keeping His commandments.[91]

---

[91] 1 John 2:3-5

Chapter 2
Educating the disciples

Matthew 10
"⁵These twelve Jesus sent forth, and commanded them, saying, Go not into the way of the Gentiles, and into any city of the Samaritans enter ye not: ⁶But go rather to the lost sheep of the house of Israel."

After the disciples received training from their Master, He gave them the opportunity to set into practice that which they had learnt. He gave them the command to go out and preach the gospel and to concentrate on the house of Israel at this time, as was predicted in the Old Testament – that the message of salvation would go firstly to the house of Israel, and later to the Gentiles.[92]

Jesus also explained this through a parable.[93] References are also made to Israel as lost sheep in the Old Testament.[94]

"⁷And as ye go, preach, saying,The kingdom of heaven is at hand."

The message:"The Kingdom of heaven/God is at hand" was first proclaimed by John the Baptist[95] and also by Jesus at the beginning of His ministry.[96]

---

[92] Dan.9:24; Rom.1:16
[93] Matt.21: 41-44
[94] Jer.50:6
[95] Matt.3:2
[96] Matt.4:17

This, also, is to be the essence of the disciples' message. Many of Jesus' teachings contained references to the kingdom of heaven, for instance "the kingdom of heaven is like… in Matt.13: 24, 31, 33, 44, 45 and 47. It also becomes evident in Jesus' later teaching, that although the kingdom of heaven was at hand during His time on earth, the fulfillment of His kingdom will be in the future.[97] This also implies that Jesus Christ is the King of this Kingdom and He will rule for all eternity.

The good news of the gospel is also contained in these words *"The Kingdom of heaven is at hand."* To accept his gift of salvation is to accept his gift of eternal life, and to be part of His kingdom forever. *"If we confess our sins, He is faithful and just to forgive us our sins and to cleanse us from all unrighteousness."* 1 John 1:9.

> *"⁸Heal the sick, cleanse the lepers, raise the dead, cast out devils: freely ye have received, freely give. ⁹Provide neither gold, nor silver, nor brass in your purses, ¹⁰Nor scrip for your journey, neither two coats, neither shoes, nor yet staves: for the workman is worthy of his meat."*

The disciples were to proclaim a message, but also to relieve the people's burdens by giving very practical assistance: to heal the sick, raising up the dead and casting out devils. Jesus spent a lot of time in healing the sick (in service of others) while He was on earth – an example to be remembered by those who go by the name of Christian today.

---

[97] Matt.24:29-44

His religion was very practical and more about relieving the burdens of others. He lived his philosophy of saving the lost and giving relief. Wherever He went there was great joy and excitement as the blind could see, the lame could walk and the deaf could hear. This was foretold by the prophet Isaiah.[98]

The disciples received very direct instructions in this regard that they were to ask no money for their services, or to take extra provisions. They were not to take extra baggage – clearly Jesus was teaching them the principle of taking one day at a time and making them rather dependent on their hosts. They had to learn to trust in God and not on their own devices.

> "[11]*And into whatsoever city or town ye shall enter, enquire who in it is worthy; and there abide till ye go thence.* [12]*And when ye come into an house, salute it.* [13]*And if the house be worthy, let your peace come upon it: but if it be not worthy, let your peace return to you.* [14]*And whosoever shall not receive you, nor hear your words, when ye depart out of that house or city, shake off the dust of your feet.* [15]*Verily I say unto you, It shall be more tolerable for the land of Sodom and Gomorrha in the day of judgment, than for that city.*"

According to verse 11 the disciples were to go to the respected people in a town and stay with them as long as was needed. This was probably to influence the town's leaders so that they could, in turn, impress the rest of the people. They were to

---

[98] Isa.61:1-3

greet the residents of the house with a salutation such as was the custom at that time, saying: Peace be to this house.[99] If they encountered a hostile home, they were to move on and leave the judgment to God. And Jesus added that judgment would fall hard on those who refused His message. By shaking off the dust of their feet, it was implied that the responsibility for that town was no longer on the disciples, but on the people themselves.

> *"[16]Behold, I send you forth as sheep in the midst of wolves: be ye therefore wise as serpents, and harmless as doves."*

The disciples were to speak the truth in love, even though this could predict trouble for them.

Jesus now emphasized certain characteristics needed by the disciples:

- sheep – gentle, following meekly after their shepherd (Jesus refers to Himself as the Good Shepherd)[100]
- serpents – alert, quick to act and to sense danger
- doves – harmless, not aggressive, innocent, genuine, not revengeful.

> *"[17]But beware of men: for they will deliver you up to the councils, and they will scourge you in their synagogues; 18And ye shall be brought before governors and kings for my sake, for a testimony against them and the Gentiles. 19But when they deliver you up, take*

---

[99] Luk.10:5
[100] John 10:1-16

no thought how or what ye shall speak: for it shall be given you in that same hour what ye shall speak. 20For it is not ye that speak, but the Spirit of your Father which speaketh in you."

Christ warned His disciples against the hidden motives of people. The persecution that Jesus talked about is that which is for His sake. In Matthew 5 He encouraged His followers by calling them "blessed" when they were being persecuted in such a way.[101] He predicted that they would be persecuted by the Sanhedrins (Jewish councils) consisting of 23 members and found in various communities. These councils had the power to punish those who trespass the law according to their own interpretation. Penalties consisting of forty floggings, at most, were administered. Usually 39 strokes were given, withholding the last one, implying mercy.

The disciples were to testify as representatives of Christ and not make up their own theories. The guidance of the Holy Spirit was promised in the giving of their testimony. The examples from the history of the disciples testifying before courts and councils, showed how the Holy Spirit endowed them with courage and wisdom when they needed it.[102]

"21And the brother shall deliver up the brother to death, and the father the child: and the children shall rise up against their parents, and cause them to be put to death. 22And ye shall be hated of all

---

[101] Matth.5:10-12
[102] Acts 4:13,31; 2 Tim.4:16,17

men for my name's sake: but he that endureth to the end shall be saved."

Christ did not predict that everything would be peaceful during our earthly existence, but to the contrary, a person's family will turn against him for accepting the Gospel of Jesus Christ. Those who proclaim the name of Jesus Christ will often be hated by others. Those who finish the race will receive the reward. To take an open stand for truth will beget opposition. We are encouraged to stand firm in our beliefs until the end.

> "*23But when they persecute you in this city, flee ye into another: for verily I say unto you, Ye shall not have gone over the cities of Israel, till the Son of man be come. 24The disciple is not above his master, nor the servant above his lord. 25It is enough for the disciple that he be as his master, and the servant as his lord. If they have called the master of the house Beelzebub, how much more shall they call them of his household.*"

As far as possible they were to move on to the next place when being persecuted. The reference to the cities of Israel here refers to the world at large, as the definition of Israel later included all God's faithful children as was explained in Hebrews 11.[103] Those who believe in Jesus Christ will be the true children of Abraham – the example of true faith in God. The disciples should always strive to be like their Master and also expect insults, because He

---

[103] Hebrews 11

was insulted. They would be accused of being from the devil as was the case with Jesus.[104]

> "[26]Fear them not therefore: for there is nothing covered, that shall not be revealed; and hid, that shall not be known. [27]What I tell you in darkness, that speak ye in light: and what ye hear in the ear, that preach ye upon the housetops."

Verse 26 refers to the fact that nothing happens on earth without God knowing about it. Everything will be revealed at the final judgment.[105]

Jesus gives the assurance that everything that needs to be heard will be heard. Everything they heard in the small group should be proclaimed to the world at large. They should not be quiet for the sake of compromise or fear. Jesus spoke the plain truth loud and clear when He was on earth. His followers should do the same.

> "[28]And fear not them which kill the body, but are not able to kill the soul: but rather fear Him which is able to destroy both soul and body in hell. [29]Are not two sparrows sold for a farthing? and one of them shall not fall on the ground without your Father. [30]But the very hairs of your head are all numbered. [31]Fear ye not therefore, ye are of more value than many sparrows."

Important are the two words: fear not, repeated in verses 26, 28 and 31 of Matthew 10. Faith in Jesus expels fear. Fear is a tool of the devil to undermine the courage of God's people. Like the disciples we

---

[104] Matt.12:24
[105] Matt.25:32

should not give fear a foothold in our lives. Many will be lost due to fear.[106] The disciples are encouraged not to be driven by fear, and especially not the fear of death. Jesus gave the assurance that those who follow Him will have everlasting life.[107] If anything is to be feared, it would be something that would destroy the soul. The Father is concerned about the sparrows and we have the assurance that nothing will happen to us which is not according to His will, when we are His children. The words:"fear Him which is able to destroy both soul and body in hell" refers to God in the final judgment.[108] God is the Creator of the earth and He will judge its inhabitants. God is and always will be in control. He is the beginning and the end. He is the great "I am." The picture of Satan, with two horns on his head, dressed in a red leotard with a pitch fork in his hand, standing amid flames is a cleverly thought out lie. People are encouraged to think that he has the power to dish out punishments, while he himself will be destroyed in the ultimate hell fires.[109] The role of the devil is to lie, to mislead and misrepresent. He is furious because he knows his ultimate fate and is jealous of those who will inherit that which he has lost.[110]

---

[106] Rev. 21:8, Matt.24:13
[107] Matt.19:16,21,29
[108] Rev.20:12-15
[109] Rev. 20:10
[110] Eze.28:14-19

The words: *"fear Him which is able to destroy both soul and body in hell"* are very important to us to expel the idea of an everlasting burning hell with Satan in control. God will ultimately destroy the wicked with fire.

> *"And whosoever was not found written in the book of life was cast into the lake of fire."* (Rev.20:15)

Man does not have an everlasting soul that will live on in hell forever. That idea does not come from the Bible, but rather from Egyptian and Greek philosophy of which the devil is the author.

If a person did not accept the gift of salvation from Jesus Christ, he will ultimately be destroyed and the results will be forever. This is one of Satan's biggest deceptions when he told Eve in the Garden of Eden: *"And the serpent said unto the woman, Ye shall not surely die"* (Genesis 3:4). And still today he and the other evil angels are misleading the people by pretending to be their deceased love ones when calling up the so-called dead. This is an abomination to the Lord and was strictly forbidden by Him in the Old Testament:

Deuteronomy 18:10-12
> *"There shall not be found among you [any one] that maketh his son or his daughter to pass through the fire, [or] that useth divination, [or] an observer of times, or an enchanter, or a witch,*
> *11 Or a charmer, or a consulter with familiar spirits, or a wizard, or a necromancer.*
> *12 For all that do these things [are] an abomination unto the LORD: and because of these abominations the LORD thy God doth drive them out from before thee."*

> *"32Whosoever therefore shall confess me before men, him will I confess also before my Father which is in heaven. 33But whosoever shall deny me before men, him will I also deny before my Father which is in heaven."*

Jesus expects loyalty from His followers and will in turn be loyal to them. To deny Christ implies a character and behavior that are contrary to His teachings,[111] for instance by speaking evil, being unclean, untruthful, selfish, uncaring, fearful and compromising truth for worldly standards.

In summary: we should not be fearful, but stand firm and always be loyal to Jesus Christ, our Redeemer.

> *"34Think not that I am come to send peace on earth: I came not to send peace, but a sword. 35For I am come to set a man at variance against his father, and the daughter against her mother, and the daughter in law against her mother in law. 36And a man's foes shall be they of his own household. 37He that loveth father or mother more than me is not worthy of me: and he that loveth son or daughter more than me is not worthy of me."*

The loyalty we demonstrate towards Jesus Christ should exceed that which we have towards our family members. This may lead to a break in our family relationships, yes even severe hatred and persecution from those who once loved us. Verse 36 also refers to Micah 7:6 in the Old Testament. Although we should honor our parents, we should

---

[111] Isa.61:1,2; Luke 4:18,19

choose God above them, if we are put to a test or forced to choose.

> "*³⁸And he that taketh not his cross, and followeth after me, is not worthy of me. ³⁹He that findeth his life shall lose it: and he that loseth his life for my sake shall find it. ⁴⁰He that receiveth you receiveth me, and he that receiveth me receiveth him that sent me. ⁴¹He that receiveth a prophet in the name of a prophet shall receive a prophet's reward; and he that receiveth a righteous man in the name of a righteous man shall receive a righteous man's reward. ⁴²And whosoever shall give to drink unto one of these little ones a cup of cold water only in the name of a disciple, verily I say unto you, he shall in no wise lose his reward."*

It is expected of the followers of Jesus to be strong and courageous, even to the point of being killed as was the case with many of God's true followers.

The disciples were to expect trouble and to be prepared for difficult times. People are unpredictable and dangerous. To lose your life for Christ's sake, leads to life everlasting. There is also a reward for those who treat His disciples with respect. Even a minor gesture of kindness to an unimportant person or child will not go unnoticed.

Matthew 11
> "*¹And it came to pass, when Jesus had made an end of commanding his twelve disciples, he departed thence to teach and to preach in their cities. ²Now when John had heard in the prison the works of Christ, he sent two of his disciples, ³And said unto him, Art thou he that should come, or do we look for another? ⁴Jesus answered and said unto them, Go and shew John again those things which ye do hear and see: ⁵The blind receive their sight, and the lame walk, the lepers are cleansed, and the deaf hear, the dead are raised up, and*

the poor have the gospel preached to them. ⁶And blessed is he, whosoever shall not be offended in me."

Jesus gave a clear and simple message to the disciples of John the Baptist: testify of the miracles that you have witnessed. As John knew the prophesies[112] he would be able to come to the right conclusions about the identity of Christ as the Messiah.

"⁷And as they departed, Jesus began to say unto the multitudes concerning John, What went ye out into the wilderness to see? A reed shaken with the wind? ⁸But what went ye out for to see? A man clothed in soft raiment? behold, they that wear soft clothing are in kings' houses. ⁹But what went ye out for to see? A prophet? yea, I say unto you, and more than a prophet. ¹⁰For this is he, of whom it is written, Behold, I send my messenger before thy face, which shall prepare thy way before thee. ¹¹Verily I say unto you, Among them that are born of women there hath not risen a greater than John the Baptist: notwithstanding he that is least in the kingdom of heaven is greater than he. ¹²And from the days of John the Baptist until now the kingdom of heaven suffereth violence, and the violent take it by force. ¹³For all the prophets and the law prophesied until John. ¹⁴And if ye will receive it, this is Elias, which was for to come. ¹⁵He that hath ears to hear, let him hear."

Jesus explained to the crowd how important John the Baptist was. He was the Elijah whose message was to proclaim the coming of the Son of God as a Savior to His people. He quoted from the Old Testament with regard to the ministry of John the Baptist.[113] Yet most of the people were ignorant,

---
[112] Isa.61:1-3;
[113] Mal 3:1

stubborn and violent – such as Herod who put John in prison and later beheaded him at the request of his daughter.

John spoke with the power of Elijah, making their sins and corruption known. He urged the people to repent. Some did so and were baptized in the Jordan River (Matt.3:2). He was preparing them for the coming Messiah, of whom the prophets spoke for many centuries, but many of them rejected John's message.

> "[16]But whereunto shall I liken this generation? It is like unto children sitting in the markets, and calling unto their fellows, [17]And saying, We have piped unto you, and ye have not danced; we have mourned unto you, and ye have not lamented. [18]For John came neither eating nor drinking, and they say, He hath a devil. [19]The Son of man came eating and drinking, and they say, Behold a man gluttonous, and a winebibber, a friend of publicans and sinners. But wisdom is justified of her children."

It is apparent that Jesus was feeling quite disappointed with the lack of understanding around Him. Although Jesus had quite a large group of people following Him, the greater majority did not take notice of the messages of John the Baptist or preaching of Jesus, but just continued with their daily lives unconcerned by what was happening under their noses. He tried to explain how people are never satisfied or receptive to truth, but would rather disqualify the message by criticizing the messenger. The community criticized John for fasting and Jesus for eating with the people. It would be wise to look at the end result of the ministries of John and Jesus – thus the fruit of wisdom. Both gained good results, even though their methods were different.

> *"Then began He to upbraid the cities wherein most of his mighty works were done, because they repented not: [21]Woe unto thee, Chorazin! woe unto thee, Bethsaida! for if the mighty works, which were done in you, had been done in Tyre and Sidon, they would have repented long ago in sackcloth and ashes. [22]But I say unto you, It shall be more tolerable for Tyre and Sidon at the day of judgment, than for you. [23]And thou, Capernaum, which art exalted unto heaven, shalt be brought down to hell: for if the mighty works, which have been done in thee, had been done in Sodom, it would have remained until this day. [24]But I say unto you, That it shall be more tolerable for the land of Sodom in the day of judgment, than for thee."*

It is quite alarming that Jesus judged whole towns at this time for their disbelief and hardened hearts. This illustrates how people can influence each other as groups which can lead to the demise of the whole group. These pronouncements must have upset the scribes and Pharisees as to the authority of Jesus to make these statements.

It is also interesting to note that according to verse 24, a final judgment still awaits Sodom. This is in accordance with Revelation 20:12-15, referring to a final judgment. Thus we are to understand that although the people of Sodom were killed by fire and brimstone, they will be resurrected again to receive their final judgment of total destruction.[114] This is referred to as the second death.

"25At that time Jesus answered and said, I thank thee, O Father, Lord of heaven and earth, because thou hast hid these things from the wise and prudent, and hast revealed them unto babes. 26Even so, Father: for so it seemed good in thy sight. 27All things are delivered unto me of my Father: and no man knoweth the Son, but the Father; neither knoweth any man the Father, save the Son, and he to whomsoever the Son will reveal him."

Once again Jesus confirmed His identity as the Son of God and thanked the Father that people of a humble character believed in Him, while those who were clever in their own eyes failed to see the truth. The leaders of Israel would not accept that Jesus Christ is the Messiah, as was predicted in the Old Testament.[115] It was in Jesus' power to reveal the true character and will of the Father to whomever He wished.

"28 Come unto me, all ye that labour and are heavy laden, and I will give you rest. 29Take my yoke upon you, and learn of me; for I am meek and lowly in heart: and ye shall find rest unto your souls. 30For my yoke is easy, and my burden is light."

Jesus had great compassion for the crowd on whose faces He could read despair, stress, distrust and fear. He knew that the human race was burdened with a sense of inner loneliness and a lack of peace. Every human being is born with a spiritual thirst that only God can fill, referred by some as a hollow inner core. By learning of Him and trusting Him, Jesus is the remedy for this

---

[114] 1Thes.4:15-17
[115] Hosea 4:6

condition of hopelessness. Through His blood He paid the penalty of sin which lay heavily on the conscience of every person.[116]

In stark contrast to Jesus' harsh words of judgment, He gave the invitation to abide in Him and He would give His followers rest for their souls. An important fact is highlighted in this section: turn your back on Jesus and face eternal damnation, or choose Him and live in peace – forever!

The persecution and problems we encounter for Christ's sake are temporal and He will provide us with the power to overcome these. We will even be able to experience inner peace despite our earthly problems by relying on his power and experiencing the presence of the Holy Spirit (also named the Comforter)[117].

The yoke that Jesus referred to is the Law of God – His standard to live by. But it will not be difficult to follow the Law of God. The scribes and Pharisees and their interpretation of the Law made it burdensome. No, He will write His law on the hearts of his followers. It will be their delight to abide by His Law.[118]

Matthew 12
"¹At that time Jesus went on the Sabbath day through the corn; and his disciples were an hungered, and began to pluck the ears of corn,

---

[116] Isa.53:6
[117] John 14:16,26
[118] Ps.40:8; Ezek.36:25-27; Ps.119:32; Heb.8:10

and to eat. ²But when the Pharisees saw it, they said unto him, Behold, thy disciples do that which is not lawful to do upon the Sabbath day. ³But he said unto them, Have ye not read what David did, when he was an hungred, and they that were with him; ⁴How he entered into the house of God, and did eat the shewbread, which was not lawful for him to eat, neither for them which were with him, but only for the priests? ⁵Or have ye not read in the law, how that on the sabbath days the priests in the temple profane the sabbath, and are blameless? ⁶But I say unto you, That in this place is one greater than the temple. ⁷But if ye had known what this meaneth, I will have mercy, and not sacrifice, ye would not have condemned the guiltless. ⁸For the Son of man is Lord even of the sabbath day."

Sometimes it seems as if Jesus transgressed the law. In such cases we should investigate a bit further, because Jesus can never contradict Himself. The discrepancy lies in our thinking. Jesus said in Matthew 5: 17:

"¹⁷Think not that I am come to destroy the law, or the prophets: I am not come to destroy, but to fulfill."

Jesus taught us to obey God's Law. The problem was the interpretation of the law by the Pharisees and scribes of the Law. They made the Law a burden to the people by adding countless extra instructions regarding the Law and especially regarding the Sabbath.[119] Jesus kept the Sabbath[120] and the rest of the Ten Commandments. He had an issue however, with the way God's Law was misinterpreted – making it a heavy burden.

---

[119] Matthew 23:13,23,24;
[120] Luke 13:10

The temple was the most sacred place on earth to the Jews. Jesus stated that He was more important than the temple. This could mean only one of two things – He was the Son of God or He was speaking blasphemy. The Pharisees could not see the truth and preferred to believe the latter. Jesus stated clearly in verse 6: *"That in this place is one greater than the temple."* The sacrificial system pointed to the perfect Sacrifice, Jesus Christ, the Lamb of God, dying on the cross on our behalf.

The philosophy behind the Law is *"mercy, more than sacrifice"*.[121] Jesus repeated this idea. He again emphasized it in Matthew 9:13 and it was also quoted in the Old Testament.[122] Another word to describe mercy is "love", as Jesus explained later in Matthew 22:37-40, where He clearly stated that the foundation on which the Law stood was love. The Pharisees' burdensome implementation of the Law misrepresented God to the people as being an unreasonable and unloving Being.

God created the Sabbath to be a delight.[123] Jesus is Lord of the Sabbath – He created the Sabbath Day for the benefit of man. The Sabbath is a special time for people to renew their relationship with their Creator, as the Sabbath was instituted at the end of creation. If you believe that the Bible is the Word of

---

[121] Matthew 23:23
[122] Hosea 6:6 & Micah 6:8
[123] Isa.58:13,14

God you have to believe in the six day creation, as in Genesis a definition is also given of a day:

> *"Gen.1:5 And God called the light Day, and the darkness he called Night. And the evening and the morning were the first day."*

When God gave Israel the Ten Commandments, He was very clear on how the Sabbath should be kept.

> **Exodus 20:**
> *"8 Remember the sabbath day, to keep it holy. 9 Six days shalt thou labour, and do all thy work: 10 But the seventh day [is] the sabbath of the LORD thy God: [in it] thou shalt not do any work, thou, nor thy son, nor thy daughter, thy manservant, nor thy maidservant, nor thy cattle, nor thy stranger that [is] within thy gates: 11 For [in] six days the LORD made heaven and earth, the sea, and all that in them [is], and rested the seventh day: wherefore the LORD blessed the sabbath day, and hallowed it."*

God did not sleep on the Sabbath, but rested.

God gave a double portion of manna on the sixth day and thereby identified to them on which day the Sabbath fell.

> *"22 And it came to pass, [that] on the sixth day they gathered twice as much bread, two omers for one [man]: and all the rulers of the congregation came and told Moses. 23 And he said unto them, This [is that] which the LORD hath said, To morrow [is] the rest of the holy sabbath unto the LORD: bake [that] which ye will bake [to day], and seethe that ye will seethe; and that which remaineth over lay up for you to be kept until the morning."*

From that time on the seventh day Sabbath was celebrated by the people of Israel. Throughout the Old Testament great emphasis was laid on the importance of the Sabbath by the prophets, e.g. Isaiah 58:13,14:

> *"13 If thou turn away thy foot from the sabbath, [from] doing thy pleasure on my holy day; and call the sabbath a delight, the holy of the LORD, honourable; and shalt honour him, not doing thine own ways, nor finding thine own pleasure, nor speaking [thine own] words: 14 Then shalt thou delight thyself in the LORD; and I will cause thee to ride upon the high places of the earth, and feed thee with the heritage of Jacob thy father: for the mouth of the LORD hath spoken [it]."*

Other Scripture references to the Sabbath in the Old Testament can be found in:

- Ex.31:13-16
- Lev.19:3,30; 26:2
- Deut.5:14
- Neh.9:14
- Isa.56:2,4,6
- Ezek.20:12,20; 22:26; 44:24

The Sabbath is an eternal institution as was prophesied by the prophet Isaiah in Isaiah 66:23, where he stated that the Sabbath will still be celebrated in heaven.

The Sabbath is also a time to celebrate our salvation in Jesus Christ.

Hebrews 4
"9 There remaineth therefore a rest to the people of God. 10 For he that is entered into his rest, he also hath ceased from his own works, as God [did] from his. 11 Let us labour therefore to enter into that rest, lest any man fall after the same example of unbelief."

The Sabbath is also a symbol of the rest that can be found in the love of God. This is a further illumination of the idea spoken in Matthew 11:28

> *"Come unto me, all ye that labour and are heavy laden, and I will give you rest."*

This was then practically demonstrated by Jesus in the following section, when Jesus showed mercy and healed someone on the Sabbath.

> *"9And when he was departed thence, he went into their synagogue: 10And, behold, there was a man which had his hand withered. And they asked him, saying, Is it lawful to heal on the sabbath days? that they might accuse him. 11And he said unto them, What man shall there be among you, that shall have one sheep, and if it fall into a pit on the sabbath day, will he not lay hold on it, and lift it out? 12How much then is a man better than a sheep? Wherefore it is lawful to do well on the sabbath days. 13Then saith he to the man, Stretch forth thine hand. And he stretched it forth; and it was restored whole, like as the other. 14Then the Pharisees went out, and held a council against him, how they might destroy him."*

Jesus knew how concerned the Pharisees and scribes would be if one of their livestock fell in a pit on a Sabbath, to quickly retrieve the animal and not suffer financial loss. They had less sympathy for human beings, though, and could not answer Jesus, but went behind His back to plot against Him. We see this phenomenon even today as people will go to great lengths to save animals such as oil-polluted penguins, but at the same time massacre hundreds of thousands of unborn human babies through abortions.

"¹⁵But when Jesus knew it, he withdrew himself from thence: and great multitudes followed him, and he healed them all; ¹⁶And charged them that they should not make him known: ¹⁷That it might be fulfilled which was spoken by Esaias the prophet, saying, ¹⁸Behold my servant, whom I have chosen; my beloved, in whom my soul is well pleased: I will put my spirit upon him, and he shall shew judgment to the Gentiles. ¹⁹He shall not strive, nor cry; neither shall any man hear his voice in the streets. ²⁰A bruised reed shall he not break, and smoking flax shall he not quench, till he send forth judgment unto victory. ²¹And in his name shall the Gentiles trust."

Matthew quoted from Isaiah,[124] showing the empathy of Jesus with the vulnerable and the suffering. During His life on earth most of His time was devoted in service of others. Jesus regards no one as inferior, but that every person can be saved by His grace.

"²²Then was brought unto him one possessed with a devil, blind, and dumb: and he healed him, insomuch that the blind and dumb both spake and saw. ²³And all the people were amazed, and said, Is not this the son of David? ²⁴But when the Pharisees heard it, they said, This fellow doth not cast out devils, but by Beelzebub the prince of the devils. ²⁵And Jesus knew their thoughts, and said unto them, Every kingdom divided against itself is brought to desolation; and every city or house divided against itself shall not stand: ²⁶And if Satan cast out Satan, he is divided against himself; how shall then his kingdom stand? ²⁷And if I by Beelzebub cast out devils, by whom do your children cast them out? therefore they shall be your judges. ²⁸But if I cast out devils by the Spirit of God, then the kingdom of God is come unto you. ²⁹Or else how can one enter into a strong man's house, and spoil his goods, except he first bind the strong man? and then he will spoil his house."

---

[124] Isa:42:1-3

After Jesus healed the demoniac, some people started to ask the question:

"Can this be the Son of David (the Messiah)?"

This angered the Pharisees and immediately they came up with a response that Jesus was working wonders through the devil.

In the great conflict between God and Satan there is no middle path of neutrality – if you are not for Jesus Christ, you are against Him. Jesus came to earth to set people free from the bondage of Satan – in other words to "bind up the strong man" and "to spoil his goods". Jesus clarified this in the following section.

> *"[30]He that is not with me is against me; and he that gathereth not with me scattereth abroad. [31]Wherefore I say unto you, All manner of sin and blasphemy shall be forgiven unto men: but the blasphemy against the Holy Ghost shall not be forgiven unto men. [32]And whosoever speaketh a word against the Son of man, it shall be forgiven him: but whosoever speaketh against the Holy Ghost, it shall not be forgiven him, neither in this world, neither in the world to come. [33]Either make the tree good, and his fruit good; or else make the tree corrupt, and his fruit corrupt: for the tree is known by his fruit. [34]O generation of vipers, how can ye, being evil, speak good things? for out of the abundance of the heart the mouth speaketh. [35]A good man out of the good treasure of the heart bringeth forth good things: and an evil man out of the evil treasure bringeth forth evil things. [36]But I say unto you, That every idle word that men shall speak, they shall give account thereof in the day of judgment. [37]For by thy words thou shalt be justified, and by thy words thou shalt be condemned."*

Stern words of reproach were spoken by Jesus about the comments made by the Pharisees. These are serious words indeed. Jesus explained to the Pharisees that their insult that He was working wonders by the devil did not hold ground as the devil would not weaken his territory by working against his own. Jesus made a very important comment that if anyone insulted the Holy Spirit, such a sin would not be forgiven. The Pharisees were increasingly rejecting the light that Jesus was indeed the Messiah, the divine Son of God, and thereby they were being led by Satan and making it impossible for them to accept Jesus as the Messiah.

The Godhead is made up of three persons: the Father, the Son (Jesus Christ) and the Holy Spirit. Their separate identities were manifested at the baptism of Jesus when the voice of God the Father spoke, and the Holy Spirit descended on Jesus like a dove (Matt.3:16, 17).

It would be a very serious mistake to ascribe the work of the Holy Spirit to be that of the devil. Caution should thus be taken in the words we so easily speak, and Jesus gave a warning in this regard in verse 37 – we will be judged by the words we speak.

A tree is known by its fruit. The idea is often repeated in the Bible that someone will be known by the fruit he bears, and this will be taken into consideration at the final judgment. If a person claims to be a converted Christian, it is to be expected that a certain mode of behavior and attitude would follow. Or else the assumption can be made that the person's conversion is fake – putting on an act without a deep spiritual change of heart (Gal.5:22).

> "³⁸Then certain of the scribes and of the Pharisees answered, saying, Master, we would see a sign from thee. ³⁹But he answered and said unto them, An evil and adulterous generation seeketh after a sign; and there shall no sign be given to it, but the sign of the prophet Jonas: ⁴⁰For as Jonas was three days and three nights in the whale's belly; so shall the Son of man be three days and three nights in the heart of the earth. ⁴¹The men of Nineveh shall rise in judgment with this generation, and shall condemn it: because they repented at the preaching of Jonas; and, behold, a greater than Jonas is here. ⁴²The queen of the south shall rise up in the judgment with this generation, and shall condemn it: for she came from the uttermost parts of the earth to hear the wisdom of Solomon; and, behold, a greater than Solomon is here."

The Pharisees and scribes asked Jesus for a sign. Already He had done so many miracles, as He explained to the disciples of John the Baptist,[125] and still they wanted a sign. He called them "an adulterous generation" which often referred to unbelieving people in the Old Testament.[126]

Jesus gave important information in this section: firstly, He foretold that He would be buried for three days and that they should take note of this when it

---

[125] Matt.11:4-6
[126] Ps.73:27

happened; Secondly, He gave credibility to the prophecies and history of the prophet Jonah. Many today dismiss the story of Jonah and the fish as a fable, but Jesus stated it as a fact. Thirdly, He told his disciples that on the Day of Judgment the following people will rise: the people of Nineveh and those who were alive at Jonah's time, and also the queen of the south. It is also important to note that all these people *"shall rise up in the judgment"*. Jesus did not proclaim anywhere that people who die will go straight to heaven or hell, although some would want to interpret sections that will be discussed later, to have this meaning. He clearly stated here that all people who died will rise up together at the judgment day. This also clearly implies that they will be "sleeping" until that time. (Joh.11:11, 14)

> *"43 When the unclean spirit is gone out of a man, he walketh through dry places, seeking rest, and findeth none. 44Then he saith, I will return into my house from whence I came out; and when he is come, he findeth it empty, swept, and garnished. 45Then goeth he, and taketh with himself seven other spirits more wicked than himself, and they enter in and dwell there: and the last state of that man is worse than the first. Even so shall it be also unto this wicked generation."*

Jesus was interrupted by someone asking a question about a sign to be given. He continued His original discourse on the sin against the Holy Spirit. Jesus warned that people should not resist the Holy Spirit's working in their hearts. Jesus shortly before this time, had set a person free from a demon (see vs. 22), and that person was probably in the audience at this time. It could be that this warning was aimed at him directly. Total commitment to God is necessary to be able to withstand the onslaught of the devil.[127] To resist evil is not enough. We should strive to live godly lives through the power of the Holy Spirit.[128]

> "[46]While he yet talked to the people, behold, his mother and his brethren stood without, desiring to speak with him. [47]Then one said unto him, Behold, thy mother and thy brethren stand without, desiring to speak with thee. [48]But he answered and said unto him that told him, Who is my mother? and who are my brethren? [49]And he stretched forth his hand toward his disciples, and said, Behold my mother and my brethren! [50]For whosoever shall do the will of my Father which is in heaven, the same is my brother, and sister, and mother."

Jesus knew people's motives and it seemed as if His brothers probably wanted to ask Him not to embarrass the family, or maybe even to warn Him of danger – as a result of His attack on the Pharisees. The brothers of Jesus probably did not believe in or understand His mission and ministry at that time.[129] At this stage He would not allow them to try and manipulate Him, by using His mother. What seemed to be rudeness to His family was actually a clear indication from Him that His mother was just an ordinary person. She was not to be revered or given special preference. He got His

---

[127] 2 Cor.6:15,16, Eph.2:22
[128] Amos 5:15, 2 Thes.2:9,10
[129] John 7:5

mandate from His heavenly Father and would not be deterred by His human family. He explained earlier on that one's family can be your enemies if they stand between you and God.[130] Jesus emphasized that those who acknowledge God as their Father belong to the family of God.[131] He did, however, care for His earthly mother as was illustrated by His words on the cross when He commissioned John to take care of her.[132]

---

[130] Matt.10:35-37, Matt.7: 21
[131] Eph.1:5
[132] Joh.19:26,27

Chapter 3

Teaching through parables

A parable is a story with the intention to teach a basic spiritual truth, often using metaphors and comparisons.

Jesus used earthly examples from everyday life to explain heavenly truths. These held their meaning throughout the ages, because He drew a line between the natural everyday experiences and understanding the divine.[133] He Himself would be the revelation of divinity – as He was more than a prophet – the Son of God. This was illustrated by the parable of the wicked husbandmen in Matthew 21:33-43. His parables were clear, short and to the point. The parables served their purpose in that it made the people curious. In his narratives Jesus used people's visual and auditory senses. The things of nature were to reflect the wisdom of the Creator.

And yet, few would be able to grasp the deeper meaning He was teaching them.[134] He had to give the explanation to the disciples (Matt.13:18-23). It was only later that they understood the full meaning (vs. 51). They questioned Jesus about his method

---

[133] Rom.1:20
[134] Matt.13:13,14

of telling parables and He quoted from Isaiah 6:9-10 (Matt.13:11 – 17).

The main reason why people could not grasp the deeper meaning of the parables, was because they could not yet grasp the meaning of the spiritual paradigm versus that of the world. Thus most of the parables in Matthew 13 start with the words *"the kingdom of heaven".* Under guidance of the Holy Spirit it will be easier for us to understand the meaning of the parables.[135] Those who sincerely long to understand His teachings will later recall the parables and better understand their meaning.

The fact remains, however, that our ears must be open to hear the voice of the Holy Spirit, and we must really and intentionally internalize this knowledge in our everyday lives. With so many untruths being spread about Jesus Christ, His character, identity and mission on earth, it becomes essential for us to pray for an open mind and open ears to be able to hear what the Spirit of God is telling us.

A variety of parables were used by Jesus to speak to various people under different circumstances of life. By using parables Jesus confused those who tried to seek His downfall.

Whereas the Sermon on the Mount seemed to be directed at the disciples, Jesus now directed His attention to the crowds. Jesus, however, explained

---

[135] John 16:13, 1Cor: 2:14

the meaning of the first parable to his disciples. This is also important for us - to counteract any misinterpretations. His explanation made it clear that He was talking about people's readiness to hear His Gospel and to act upon it.

In Matthew 13:17 Jesus tried to explain to his disciples how privileged they were to hear the teachings spoken by Him, the Son of God, and how many people in years gone by would have marveled at such a privilege.

Parable number 1

Matthew 13
"1 The same day went Jesus out of the house, and sat by the sea side. 2And great multitudes were gathered together unto him, so that he went into a ship, and sat; and the whole multitude stood on the shore. 3And he spake many things unto them in parables, saying, Behold, a sower went forth to sow; 4And when he sowed, some seeds fell by the way side, and the fowls came and devoured them up: 5Some fell upon stony places, where they had not much earth: and forthwith they sprung up, because they had no deepness of earth: 6And when the sun was up, they were scorched; and because they had no root, they withered away. 7And some fell among thorns; and the thorns sprung up, and choked them: 8But other fell into good ground, and brought forth fruit, some an hundredfold, some sixtyfold, some thirtyfold. 9Who hath ears to hear, let him hear.
10And the disciples came, and said unto him, Why speakest thou unto them in parables? 11He answered and said unto them, Because it is given unto you to know the mysteries of the kingdom of heaven, but to them it is not given. 12For whosoever hath, to him shall be given, and he shall have more abundance: but whosoever hath not, from him shall be taken away even that he hath. 13Therefore speak I to them in parables: because they seeing see not; and hearing they hear not, neither do they understand. 14And in them is fulfilled the

prophecy of Esaias, which saith, By hearing ye shall hear, and shall not understand; and seeing ye shall see, and shall not perceive: [15]For this people's heart is waxed gross, and their ears are dull of hearing, and their eyes they have closed; lest at any time they should see with their eyes, and hear with their ears, and should understand with their heart, and should be converted, and I should heal them. [16]But blessed are your eyes, for they see: and your ears, for they hear. [17]For verily I say unto you, That many prophets and righteous men have desired to see those things which ye see, and have not seen them; and to hear those things which ye hear, and have not heard them."

Jesus' own explanation of parable number 1

"[18]Hear ye therefore the parable of the sower. [19]When any one heareth the word of the kingdom, and understandeth it not, then cometh the wicked one, and catcheth away that which was sown in his heart. This is he which received seed by the way side. [20]But he that received the seed into stony places, the same is he that heareth the word, and anon with joy receiveth it; [21]Yet hath he not root in himself, but dureth for a while: for when tribulation or persecution ariseth because of the word, by and by he is offended. [22]He also that received seed among the thorns is he that heareth the word; and the care of this world, and the deceitfulness of riches, choke the word, and he becometh unfruitful. [23]But he that received seed into the good ground is he that heareth the word, and understandeth it; which also beareth fruit, and bringeth forth, some an hundredfold, some sixty, some thirty."

The sower, the seed and the soil

Jesus gave an extensive explanation of the meaning of this parable. It was beneficial for his disciples that He gave the explanation thereof right away. This would help them to understand that when He referred to the kingdom of heaven, He was talking about spiritual and not material things (agricultural gain).

The sower: The same sower goes out in all four cases and he sows the same seed. The difference lies in the acceptance of the seed by the four kinds of soil. Jesus is the sower of the seed. It was his mission to reveal the truth about God and sow the seeds of wisdom and true knowledge. If a person sincerely seeks to know the truth revealed by God, his prayers will be answered.[136] After Jesus ascended into heaven this role would go to his disciples and followers, [137] aided by the Holy Spirit.

The seed: The seed is the Word of God. The words of God are contained in the Bible which we refer to in general as the Word of God. The uncontaminated Word, including the good news of the Gospel, should be spread to everyone on earth.[138] The Word of God was, and still is, under constant attack from the devil and his helpers. Learned people think themselves elevated above the truth of the Bible. They question its authority and they try to explain away basic truths, and attempt to translate away the fundamental truths of the Bible.[139] Everyone should study the Bible for themselves and not depend on others to do so for them. It is within everyone's reach. The time has passed to trust the words of

---

[136] John 7:17; 1John 1:1-3
[137] Matt.28:19,20
[138] 2Tim.4:2; 2 Pet.1:16
[139] 2Tim.4:3,4; Prov.30:5,6

others, be they professors, doctors in Theology, priests or pastors. Jesus Himself often quoted from the Scriptures available at the time, namely from the Old Testament. See the Introduction as to determine from which specific books He quoted.

According to this parable it might seem as if some people cannot be blamed for their own ignorance, e.g. the seed that fell on the way side and stony places. But as Jesus Himself explained in Matt. 13:19 – 22, these conditions exist in the hearts of man when there is no depth of understanding, and no real interest in the Word of God. Worldly influences and attractions, allow the devil to neutralize God's Word. Ignorance of God's Word therefore, is not an excuse! The people in the time of Jesus could not understand his mission, as it was not according to their expectations. They could not recognize the Son of God in their midst. Jesus explained to the disciples of John the Baptist that the signs were clear, indicating that He was the Messiah they were waiting for (Matt.11:4-6):

> "Go and shew John again those things which ye do hear and see: *5The blind receive their sight, and the lame walk, the lepers are cleansed, and the deaf hear, the dead are raised up, and the poor have the gospel preached to them. 6And blessed is he, whosoever shall not be offended in me."

Still most people doubted that He was indeed the long-awaited Messiah.

Some seed fell by the wayside: These people are those who hear but do not listen and obey. They do not give their full attention. Their spiritual capabilities are shallow as they are too absorbed with the things of the world. They cannot identify their spiritual loneliness and the aimlessness of their lives – an emptiness that only Jesus can fill. The evil one easily distracts them from the truths of the Word when they hear it. They criticize the shortcomings of the preacher and immediately sow doubt and unbelief. This was demonstrated by the birds coming down and devouring the seed right away.

Some seed fell in stony places: In this case the shallow layer of earth is underlined by solid rock. Again, self is more important than anything else. This category of people seems to be easily persuaded. There is always joy in heaven when a sinner repents.[140] Unfortunately their good intentions do not last long. As soon as they come across any form of opposition they give up. As soon as some realize that their commitment to Jesus would ask of them to give up some sinful habits or practices, they reconsider. The price for them is too high. They have no real relationship with Jesus, and do not depend on Him for divine help to overcome their bad habits. They cannot see the eternal value of Jesus' love, but would rather conform to present conveniences. It is asking too

---

[140] Luke 15:7

much of them to humble themselves and commit themselves fully to Jesus Christ and His cause. These cannot stand up when they are confronted by temptation or mockers. They cannot pass the test of self-sacrifice and denial. In retrospect, however, it is apparent that Jesus did die for all men. It is through their hardness of heart[141] that many do not want to accept the grace offered to them – as a result of their own pride and self-sufficiency.

Some seed fell among thorns: In the case of the seed that fell among the thorns, it is clear that some people would act upon the hearing of the Gospel impulsively - to easily accept a new truth. Their lives are however crowded by many other thoughts and actions. If we do not weed our gardens, the flowers or vegetables cannot grow. They are soon overtaken by weeds. Our hearts must constantly be purified to accept the truth of the Word. As soon as other thoughts of material riches or worries become more important than God's Word and we cannot find time to grow spiritually, then we fall into this category. We can become so preoccupied with the concerns of this world that we lose the vision of Jesus' soon return.[142]

Some seed fell on good ground: A person with a good heart is not a person without sin, but one who listens to the prompting of the Holy Spirit. Jesus is available to those who feel their spiritual need.[143]

---

[141] Heb.3:13; Eze.36:26,27
[142] Luke 21:34-36

Good ground represents the one who has faith.[144] It also represents those who eagerly accept the word of God as truth.[145] Furthermore, these people are willing to accept and obey the commandments of God.[146] The good ground, the fertile soil, represents those who have an honest purpose – to be like Christ and to do His will.[147] As was the case with the other soil/ hearers of the Word, the Word confronts these hearers. They are set before the test to either follow Jesus in total commitment or fall back on old habits. In full co-operation with the Holy Spirit they lay down their old lives and become new people who bring forth the fruit of the Spirit.[148] Conflict does not bear these people down, but strengthens their faith.[149] The "good ground" people are looking forward to the coming of the Lord.[150] While they wait they deliver a harvest of a good crop.[151] The fruit referred to are the souls which they lead to the Lord. In some cases it will be 30 times, 60 times or 100 times as Jesus said. The impact they have on their world to bring the good news of the gospel will depend largely on their openness to the guiding of the Holy Spirit. He encourages us to live whole-

---

[143] Mark2:17; 1 John1:9
[144] Heb.11:6; Eph.2:8
[145] 1 Thes.2:13; Matt.5:6
[146] 1 John 2:3-6
[147] Ps.40:8;1 John 2:6
[148] Gal.5:22-25
[149] James 1:12
[150] James 5:7,8
[151] John 14:12

heartedly for Him, and produce a great harvest of fruit for His kingdom.

Parable number 2

"24Another parable put he forth unto them, saying, The kingdom of heaven is likened unto a man which sowed good seed in his field: 25But while men slept, his enemy came and sowed tares among the wheat, and went his way. 26But when the blade was sprung up, and brought forth fruit, then appeared the tares also. 27So the servants of the householder came and said unto him, Sir, didst not thou sow good seed in thy field? from whence then hath it tares? 28 He said unto them, An enemy hath done this. The servants said unto him, Wilt thou then that we go and gather them up? 29But he said, Nay; lest while ye gather up the tares, ye root up also the wheat with them. 30Let both grow together until the harvest: and in the time of harvest I will say to the reapers, Gather ye together first the tares, and bind them in bundles to burn them: but gather the wheat into my barn."

Jesus' explanation of parable number 2

"36Then Jesus sent the multitude away, and went into the house: and his disciples came unto him, saying, Declare unto us the parable of the tares of the field.
37He answered and said unto them, He that soweth the good seed is the Son of man; 38 The field is the world; the good seed are the children of the kingdom; but the tares are the children of the wicked one; 39 The enemy that sowed them is the devil; the harvest is the end of the world; and the reapers are the angels. 40As therefore the tares are gathered and burned in the fire; so shall it be in the end of this world. 41The Son of man shall send forth his angels, and they shall gather out of his kingdom all things that offend, and them which do iniquity; 42And shall cast them into a furnace of fire: there shall be wailing and gnashing of teeth. 43Then shall the righteous shine forth

as the sun in the kingdom of their Father. Who hath ears to hear, let him hear."

The tares and the wheat

This parable was also explained by Jesus. Most writers agree that the tares probably refer to the bearded darnel which grows in Palestine and resembles wheat whilst growing, except that it turns black when it matures, and is poisonous.

We understand "the field" to be the church represented throughout the world. The good seed is the children of God, as Jesus explained. The tares are those who join the church with hidden agendas and impure motives - those who spread falsehood, disunity and strife within the church. Satan is the one who sows the tares. These so-called "Christians" want to be members of the church for obscure and devious reasons, but they do not represent the true character of a Christian, nor bear the fruit of the Spirit.

The tares make things difficult for the children of God and they sometimes wish that they could rid themselves of these troublesome people. Although the church should not tolerate people who stubbornly and openly sin, they do not have the right to judge other's characters or motives. Those who are struggling to understand the principles of the Kingdom of heaven might still be reached someday by the power of God.[152] Jesus taught us to be forgiving and merciful.[153] While the tares grow closely to the wheat, the wheat might also be uprooted when the tares are pulled out. In the same way, if we deal harshly with others in our church, this might upset other sensitive or young believers. Let them be, in time God will be the judge of everyone's character. He knows everyone's heart and with time everyone will reveal themselves according to their works. We should let God deal with the tares.

It is also interesting to note that the tares will grow with the wheat until the end of time. Nowhere is there a 100% pure church to be found, or one single denomination of whom all members will inherit eternal life.

In the past, civil and religious powers were used to destroy the so-called heretics in the church. These actions are inspired by the devil and do not come from God. He will come on the clouds of heaven with His judgment when the time is ripe.[154] He alone knows everything and can be a fair judge of all.[155] At that time people cannot change anymore – their true character will be clear for all to see.[156] In Matthew 25 we read that they are separated into two categories: sheep and goats and they are

---

[152] Zech.3:2,12,13-20
[153] Matt.9:13
[154] Matt.25:31-33
[155] Mal.3:18
[156] Rev.22:11,12

classified as such by their works. Those who truly accept Jesus as their Savior will have done the works that He wanted them to do as a natural outflow of their love for Him.[157] Eventually, at the end the wicked will be destroyed - cast into a furnace of fire.

Parable number 3

> "31 Another parable put he forth unto them, saying, The kingdom of heaven is like to a grain of mustard seed, which a man took, and sowed in his field: 32 Which indeed is the least of all seeds: but when it is grown, it is the greatest among herbs, and becometh a tree, so that the birds of the air come and lodge in the branches thereof. "

A mustard seed

Jesus and His teaching was dismissed by many of the bystanders, including many scribes and Pharisees, as being insignificant. They judged Him by worldly standards. He did not have any material riches or status to impress. By His words and the miracles He performed, people were to recognize Him as the Messiah.

Through the parable of the mustard seed, He was telling them that, despite the humble beginnings of His kingdom, it will grow into something cosmic. For centuries the church of God would grow and grow and accumulate millions of people. The church is open to all who accept the truth of God and His word, like a tree providing shelter and shade to

---

[157] Matt.24:31-46

birds. Humble followers enthused by the Holy Spirit and the truth of God's word, will achieve more to spread the gospel of the kingdom of heaven than the important people, the wealthy, the learned, and the celebrities of this world.[158]

Within a seed is hidden the possibility of life and growth, such as only God can provide. Every seed develops into a new creation, according to its own nature. A seed can grow into a wonderful tree without human intervention. So it will be with God's true church. It will grow and nothing will be able to stop it. It cannot be stopped through brutal power, even when this approach was tried during the Dark Ages.

The Jews hoped for a leader who would overthrow the Roman government and they were not impressed with the humble appearance of Jesus. They were too materialistic to grasp the spiritual meaning of the Kingdom of Heaven. They were, however, warned by the prophet Isaiah[159] about His humble appearance, and still only a few were sharp enough to understand and accept the writings of the Old Testament.

Parable number 4

> "*33Another parable spake he unto them; The kingdom of heaven is like unto leaven, which a woman took, and hid in three measures of meal, till the whole was leavened.*

---

[158] 1 Cor.1:26-28; 1 Cor.2:5
[159] Isa.53:2

34All these things spake Jesus unto the multitude in parables; and without a parable spake he not unto them: 35That it might be fulfilled which was spoken by the prophet, saying, I will open my mouth in parables; I will utter things which have been kept secret from the foundation of the world."

Leaven

The symbol of leaven was sometimes used to illustrate the working of sin.[160]

In this parable, however, the kingdom of heaven is illustrated as leaven and the quickening power of the Holy Spirit that works from the inside out.

When a person submits to the Holy Spirit, a new power is activated and the lost image of God is restored. A person cannot transform him-/herself on their own, but Someone greater than themselves must do this for him or her. This is where the grace of God comes in.[161] We must receive His grace before we are fit for His kingdom. The change and the renewing energy must come from the Holy Spirit. Worldly knowledge and personal intelligence will not bring about a change of heart. Grace is a gift from God bestowed on those who sincerely long for it.[162]

No matter how hard we try to be good, to kick old habits, we cannot succeed when we rely on our own strength. Our hearts must be converted and

---

[160] Luk.12:1; 1 Cor.5:8
[161] Eph.2:4-8
[162] Matt.11:25-27

sanctified. If we try to keep God's commandments out of a sense of obligation, obedience will be a burden. True obedience is the result of the Holy Spirit working from within. We love God because He loved us first and this leads to a love for the law, a longing to do God's will.[163]

Like leaven, the working of the Holy Spirit is invisible. Slowly we are endowed with traits of character that will enable us to be of service to God.

This kind of conversion was illustrated by the words of Jesus to Nicodemus in John 3:3-8 when Jesus explained to Nicodemus that he should be born again.

Many claim to be Christians, but their works testify against them. Their behavior, speech and thoughts reflect that they have not yet experienced an inward change by the Holy Spirit.

Faith is based on hearing and obeying the Word of God.[164] The Holy Spirit and the Word work together to bring us the truth and to convict us of sin.[165] The principles of the Bible should be practiced daily in our lives and permeate our thoughts, feelings and actions. We can only succeed in fulfilling this aim through the working of the Holy Spirit. The leaven of truth subdues our worldly and selfish desires, purifies our thoughts and softens our hearts. It

---

[163] Ps.119:1,2,10,11,18,32; 1John.2:3,4
[164] Rom.10:17
[165] John 17:17

enlarges our capacity for compassion and empathy, as well as quickening the capacity of mind and soul.

This attitude and conduct are contrary to the standards of the world where selfish ambition, greed and corruption reign.

The love that is from God is not selfish or changeable, nor does it depend on human praise. It is summarized by Paul in 1 Cor.13:4-7 where he states: *"Love suffers long and is kind; love does not envy; love does not parade itself, is not puffed up; does not behave rudely, does not seek its own, is not provoked, thinks no evil; does not rejoice in iniquity, but rejoices in the truth; bears all things, believes all things, hopes all things, endures all things."* (New King James Version)

Christians are to live holy as God is holy – that is: consecrated to the service of God.[166]

Parable number 5

"⁴⁴Again, the kingdom of heaven is like unto treasure hid in a field; the which when a man hath found, he hideth, and for joy thereof goeth and selleth all that he hath, and buyeth that field."

Hidden Treasure

It was customary in ancient times for people to bury treasure in the earth. Later the place of the burial could be forgotten or the owner killed. In this way someone might come across a hidden treasure by accident. In the parable a man, whilst cultivating the land, unearthed buried treasure. He put it back, sold all that he owned and bought the field.

---

[166] 1 Pet.1:13-16

The parable illustrates the value of the heavenly treasure. The finder of the treasure was willing to part with all his possessions, and invest in untiring labor to secure this treasure. So the finder of heavenly treasure will go to great lengths and be willing to sacrifice everything of earthly value to find the treasures of truth.

In this parable the field represents the Holy Scriptures, and the gospel of redemption through Jesus Christ is the treasure. There are many precious things to be found in the Scriptures. The truth of the gospel is said to be hidden from those who are wise in their own eyes. Even in Christ's days His people did not recognize Him for what He was because of their preconceived ideas, traditions and own interpretation of the Scripture.

God does not hide His truth from people. Because Christ, as well as His forerunner, John the Baptist, called for a change in their life style, they turned their backs on Him. Pride made it impossible for them to acknowledge their own erroneous thinking. They rejected the greatest gift ever offered to them. They were too concerned about what others would say if they confessed Him.[167]

The people of today have the same problem: searching for earthly riches and values, having thoughts centered on selfish ambition, they miss the point of the message contained in Scripture and as

---

[167] John 12:42,43

such the true message thereof is hidden to them.[168] It is by being blind to the truth through their own hardness of heart that the treasure of the Bible is hidden to many.

This was one of the main themes of Jesus' teaching – for people to look away from the material world to the spiritual.[169] True riches are buried in the Word of God and its value is above that of gold or silver.[170] God knows everything as He is the Creator of everything. By studying His Word under the guidance of the Holy Spirit, He will unveil to us all the truths of creation and salvation. The Bible is the only book containing the uncompromised plain truth.[171]

The paradox of the wisdom of God is that He can reveal its truth to the simplest of minds, while it eludes the learned and wise of the world. No matter how much time we spend in studying at universities and colleges gaining one degree after the other, it will not compare to the knowledge of the Word of God and His revealed will that will bring us salvation and peace.[172] It is not "what" we know, but "Who" we know!

Every person should dig for truth for himself and herself. There are many levels of understanding the

---

[168] 1 Cor.2:14
[169] Matt.16:26
[170] Job 28: 12-18
[171] 1 Pet.1:10,11; 1 Cor.2:13,14
[172] 1 Cor.1:20,30

Word. Scanning the surface, rummaging through the chapters, acting hastily due to a feeling of obligation, these will not bring about spiritual growth. Some people depend on the interpretation of others and are too lazy to search the truth for themselves. Without the guidance and interpretation of the Holy Spirit, some will make wrong assumptions – reading what they want to hear and not what the Bible is saying. Human theories do not lead to a better understanding of the Word. It is through this avenue that many false teachings started. Even in the days of Jesus people relied on the teachings of the Pharisees instead of the Scriptures. Jesus reprimanded them for doing so.[173] They thought that they had great wisdom but Jesus said to them that they do not know Scripture and that they were teaching the commandments of men.[174] Earnest prayer to God to direct our thoughts and minds enlightening us through the power of the Holy Spirit, is the only way to find the hidden treasures of the Word.[175]

Those who long to know the truth should be prepared to put some diligent effort into the study of God's Word. In the parable the man sold all his other belongings. He had a singular goal on which he focused with everything he had. Others must

---

[173] Mark 12:24
[174] Mark 7:7-9
[175] 1 Cor.12:8-11; Heb.4:12,13

have thought that he was mad, but he was motivated by the reward that he could envisage.

It is for our own personal benefit that we need to know the contents of the Bible – for our own salvation and spiritual growth. We need to ascertain God's will for us. Our response to the Word should be that of obedience. Our knowledge of the Bible should assist us into the right relationship with God. We should humble ourselves, bow low before Him and listen to what He wants from us. He is our Creator and we His creation.[176] We should learn to stop depending on our own resources and be totally committed to Him.[177] To be able to do this we must listen to the Word of God and put away our own ideas and interpretations. To read the Bible with the wrong motives, such as to vindicate our own ideas, will not bring us anywhere. Without faith we cannot earnestly search or find the gospel truth.[178]

It is the work of the Holy Spirit to assist us in making the right interpretations. If two people interpret Scripture totally different, it will probably be correct to assume that either one or both did not follow the guidance of the Holy Spirit but relied on their own "wisdom".

It is one of the wonders of the Word that no one can ever stop learning from it. There are deeper levels

---

[176] John 1:1-3
[177] Ps.119:1-16; Matt.6:33
[178] John 3:3,15-17

of truths to discover beyond superficial reading which is not easy to grasp at first. Prayerful meditation on Scripture will open new avenues and deeper meanings that will amaze and quicken the soul. Great riches will be the reward of the person who is willing to commit him- or herself totally to the searching of Scripture - to read and follow attentively as an obedient child. This kind of knowledge will impart power that will enable us to live and grow daily into the image that God has foreseen for us at our creation.[179] This kind of knowledge contains truth that will secure eternal life for us.[180] This kind of knowledge is within the reach of everyone one who earnestly seeks for it.[181]

Parable number 6

> "[45]Again, the kingdom of heaven is like unto a merchant man, seeking goodly pearls: [46]Who, when he had found one pearl of great price, went and sold all that he had, and bought it."

The parable begins with the word "again" indicating that the same principles are applicable in this parable as in the parable of the hidden treasure.

A truly good pearl of great price is something precious and of great beauty. Christ is the pearl of great price. On earth He shone forth in purity, brilliance and splendor.[182] A pearl of great price is

---

[179] John 17:3
[180] John 11:25,26
[181] Prov.2:2-5; Luk.11:9
[182] Matt.17:2;

one without spot or blemish, as was Jesus who never sinned. Pearls have a wonderful shine, glowing in the light, as Jesus is the light.[183] The glory and brightness of the Father is expressed in His character. [184]He is the the light and He receives it from the Father. All that we could ever need is found in Jesus Christ. Salvation in Jesus is far more valuable than anything this world can offer.[185]

Like the merchantman those who desire the real thing must give up all else in order to acquire the pearl of great price. Jesus paid the ultimate price for our salvation on the cross of Calvary. We should totally surrender ourselves to Christ in return: body, soul and spirit. We have to be wholly consecrated to His service.[186] Then we obtain the pearl of great price through obedience to His Word. This invitation is extended to all.[187]Some people of the world consider themselves rich, without realizing that they are indeed spiritually poor.[188]

We cannot earn salvation, but if we are sincere and love the Lord with all our heart, we will strive to be with God. We will persevere in our quest for eternal life and live in obedience to His Word. We will do His will because of our love for Him and our thankfulness, because He died for us. If we live

---

[183] John 8:12;
[184] 1 John 1:5
[185] 1 John 2:16,17; Col.2:2; 1 Cor.1:30
[186] Rom.12:1,2
[187] Rev.3:8,18,20
[188] Rev.3:17

lives to serve our own selfish purposes we will not inherit the Kingdom of Heaven. We only bluff ourselves by belonging to churches which are to us nothing but social clubs, while we refuse to give up our sinful habits and/or self-righteousness. Yes, there is a price to pay. We have to deny ourselves and take up the cross daily.[189] We cannot expect Christ to die for us and from our side follow our own pursuits of worldly riches. We were not placed on earth to be entertained, but to serve.[190] He created us and gave us life, to give us a chance to inherit the eternal Kingdom and to live as the perfect beings that He originally intended for us to be.[191] In heaven we will have the perfect fellowship with God as was originally intended at creation.[192]

The parable of the pearl of great price could have a double meaning. It could also mean that Christ came to earth to seek for us – His lost creation. Through Christ we can be redeemed.[193] He paid a great price for our salvation.

The Holy Spirit reveals to us the preciousness and beauty of the pearl of great price.[194] After the outpouring of the Holy Spirit, Jesus' followers grasped the true meaning of salvation in Jesus and their faith was thus strengthened.[195]

---

[189] Rom.8:35-39; Matt.16:24
[190] Matt.10:22,38,39,
[191] John 11:25,26
[192] Rev.21:3
[193] Zech.9:16; Mal.3:17; Heb.7:25; John 1:12
[194] Rom.8:14

The character of Christ was reflected by the members of the early church after they received the illuminating gift of the Holy Spirit as light was reflected in a valuable pearl.[196] We are waiting for the latter rain (a special endowment of the Holy Spirit) to be poured out and strengthen us for the end-time. [197] That is the time directly before the second coming of Jesus Christ, foretold by him in Matthew 24.

Parable number 7

> *"[47] Again, the kingdom of heaven is like unto a net, that was cast into the sea, and gathered of every kind: [48] Which, when it was full, they drew to shore, and sat down, and gathered the good into vessels, but cast the bad away. [49] So shall it be at the end of the world: the angels shall come forth, and sever the wicked from among the just, [50] And shall cast them into the furnace of fire: there shall be wailing and gnashing of teeth [51] Jesus saith unto them, Have ye understood all these things? They say unto him, Yea, Lord."*

The Net

The casting of the net symbolizes the preaching of the gospel. It gathers the good and the bad into His kingdom.

Again we are shown a picture of judgment at the end of time. This parable confirms the fact that there will be evil people and false Christians until the end. These people will bring the name of Christ

---

[195] Acts 5:31,32; John 8:12
[196] Acts 4:32,33
[197] Zech.10:1

into disrepute. They will turn against their fellow believers and be a stumbling block to many. But to God they are easily identifiable. At the end a person's character will give him/her away and confirm the fact that not all who call themselves Christians, were truly converted or controlled by the Holy Spirit.[198] After judgment there will be no more chance for conversion, and destruction of the wicked will follow. Those who do not respond to his pleading will perish. Those who cling to sin will perish.[199] Yet it is God's wish that everyone of His creation be converted.[200]

Parable number 8

> *"[52]Then said he unto them, Therefore every scribe which is instructed unto the kingdom of heaven is like unto a man that is an householder, which bringeth forth out of his treasure things new and old."*

Things old and new

In this parable Jesus referred to persons called to teach others of the kingdom of heaven, such as his disciples. Such persons would draw insight from the Scriptures, both from the Old Testament, which existed in the days of Jesus and from the New Testament which was in the making.[201] He could foresee the Word being available to His followers in

---

[198] Rom.8:8,9; Matt.7:21
[199] Rom.6:23
[200] Ezek.33:11; John 3:17
[201] Hebr.11:1-3; Ps.33:3,9

written form in the future, even after His death. The treasure of wisdom and insight which His disciples have gained are to be "brought out" and communicated to others desiring to know the truth of salvation.

Jesus Himself quoted often from the Old Testament books available in His time. According to Matthew, Jesus quoted from: Isaiah, Micah, Hosea, Jeremiah, Deuteronomy, Psalms, Exodus, Leviticus, Malachi, Genesis, Zechariah and Daniel. John also mentioned Nehemiah. The book of Acts, which deals with the history of the early church, mentioned Joel, Samuel, Habakkuk and Amos. The Old Testament prophets foretold the coming of the Messiah.[202] They spoke of His birth, life and death. The sacrificial offering system pointed to Christ's sacrifice on the cross.[203]

Everybody who finds this treasure of the Good News will long to share it with others, like a child who enthusiastically wants to show off the wonderful presents that he got for his birthday. It is impossible to keep these precious life-giving truths to oneself.

The Word of God is like a great treasure chest of which the value and depths can never be fathomed. The more a person searches, the more his knowledge increases and as the Holy Spirit leads,

---

[202] Isa. 53;
[203] Ps.40:6-8

the more he/she becomes changed into the likeness of Christ. The Bible is also a testimony of how God led his people in the past. It illustrates the consequences of the working of the Holy Spirit in the lives of the prophets in the Old Testament and the members of the early church.

The Old and New Testaments should be read together for a deeper understanding of the will of God.[204] The law (which is the reflection of the character of God) points to man's inability to be obedient and his dire need for a Savior, whilst salvation through faith in Christ provides the answer to this dilemma.[205]

Studying Scripture is like a never-ending treasure hunt. It will enrich our lives and nurture our spiritual growth. Our understanding and appreciation for our own salvation through the blood of the Lamb, Jesus Christ, will ever increase. We should live and grow by his Word – He is the Living Bread and His blood is the Living Water. We should study prayerfully for the guidance of the Holy Spirit to illuminate and interpret Scripture to us.

Main themes of the parables: The kingdom of heaven is like....

---

[204] John 5:39
[205] Eph.2:8-10

TABLE 5   MAIN THEMES OF THE PARABLES

Theme of parable	Meaning of parable
1. The sower, the seed and the soil	The reception of God's word by different classes of hearers and the subsequent results.
2. The tares and the wheat	There will be two classes of people in the church. It is not our duty to separate the tares from the wheat. They will eventually reveal their true colors and be judged accordingly by God.
3. A mustard seed	The church of God will grow extensively, despite its humble beginnings.
4. Leaven	An illustration of the inner workings and growth in the life of a believer/ the church through the working of the Holy Spirit.
5. Hidden treasure	The intention and effort of one who searches for truth will be satisfied.
6. A pearl of great price	The saving grace of Jesus Christ is of the greatest value – far more important than anything else in life.
7. A fishing net	The good and bad will finally be separated.
8. Things old and new	The Word of God will be our treasure chest

In summary it can be said that from these parables we are to understand that:

- Not everyone will be ready to accept the good news of salvation through Jesus Christ the Anointed Messiah.

- The devil will do his best to upset the unity of the church by encouraging people with impure motives to join the church.
- Nevertheless the committed individual and church will grow extensively if rooted in God and his Word and will be a safe haven for many.
- The working of the Holy Spirit can be witnessed and experienced, but not explained.
- To the individual who finds this truth, it will be the most important aspect and become the first priority in his life.
- There will be an ultimate judgment when the good and the bad will be separated and the wicked will be destroyed by fire, whilst the good will inherit the kingdom of heaven.

Malachi 4
"¹For, behold, the day cometh, that shall burn as an oven; and all the proud, yea, and all that do wickedly, shall be stubble: and the day that cometh shall burn them up, saith the LORD of hosts, that it shall leave them neither root nor branch. ⁰But unto you that fear my name shall the Sun of righteousness arise with healing in his wings; and ye shall go forth, and grow up as calves of the stall. ³ And ye shall tread down the wicked; for they shall be ashes under the soles of your feet in the day that I shall do [this], saith the LORD of hosts."

- Studying the Word of God will feed us, sustain us and enable us to grow spiritually.

Jesus made use of more parables to illuminate matters to the scribes and Pharisees, as will be illustrated in the next chapter.

Chapter 4

Jesus answers trick questions

Matthew 15:1-20
"¹Then came to Jesus scribes and Pharisees, which were of Jerusalem, saying, ²Why do thy disciples transgress the tradition of the elders? for they wash not their hands when they eat bread. ³But he answered and said unto them, Why do ye also transgress the commandment of God by your tradition? ⁴For God commanded, saying, Honour thy father and mother: and, He that curseth father or mother, let him die the death. ⁵But ye say, Whosoever shall say to his father or his mother, It is a gift, by whatsoever thou mightest be profited by me; ⁶And honour not his father or his mother, he shall be free. Thus have ye made the commandment of God of none effect by your tradition. ⁷Ye hypocrites, well did Esaias prophesy of you, saying, ⁸This people draweth nigh unto me with their mouth, and honoureth me with their lips; but their heart is far from me. ⁹But in vain they do worship me, teaching for doctrines the commandments of men.
¹⁰And he called the multitude, and said unto them, Hear, and understand: ¹¹Not that which goeth into the mouth defileth a man; but that which cometh out of the mouth, this defileth a man."

A deputation of scribes and Pharisees questioned Jesus in order to find anything that they could accuse him of.

An accusation was made because the disciples did not wash their hands before eating bread. The Pharisees had endless purification rituals and regulations formed by their own tradition. These were put above the Law of God in many instances.

Jesus did not answer them by defending his disciples, but by showing the scribes and Pharisees an example of how they circumvented the Law which stated that you should honor your father and mother. This was one of the Ten Commandments which God himself wrote with his finger on tables of stone. The people were encouraged to devote their property to the temple by the Jewish authorities and this duty was seen as more important than the duty towards mother and father. According to this tradition a child could pronounce the word "corban" over his property and in this manner devote it to the Temple. His parents could thus be defrauded if anything happened to the child.

Jesus inspired people to pay their tithes and offerings to the temple. The priests and rabbis were anxious to build an empire for themselves and thus imposed heavy burdens and taxes on the people. Jesus quoted from the prophet Isaiah in this regard.[206] He turned to the crowd and again emphasized the foulness of our words and how what came out of our mouths could have dire consequences.

> "*12Then came his disciples, and said unto him, Knowest thou that the Pharisees were offended, after they heard this saying? 13But he answered and said, Every plant, which my heavenly Father hath not planted, shall be rooted up. 14Let them alone: they be blind leaders of the blind. And if the blind lead the blind, both shall fall into the ditch.*

---

[206] Isa.29:13

15Then answered Peter and said unto him, Declare unto us this parable. 16And Jesus said, Are ye also yet without understanding? 17Do not ye yet understand, that whatsoever entereth in at the mouth goeth into the belly, and is cast out into the draught? 18But those things which proceed out of the mouth come forth from the heart; and they defile the man. 19For out of the heart proceed evil thoughts, murders, adulteries, fornications, thefts, false witness, blasphemies: 20These are the things which defile a man: but to eat with unwashen hands defileth not a man."

Jesus explained that every teaching or tradition not founded in God's Word will be uprooted when He comes to judge the world.[207] We should be careful not to prefer human authority, church traditions or customs above the Word of God. He referred to the Pharisees and scribes as blind leaders, leading the blind. In their midst was the Messiah whom they had waited for, for centuries, and yet they did not recognize Him.

In his explanation Jesus spoke about the defilement that comes from within – evil thoughts leading to murder, adultery, fornication, thefts, false witness and blasphemy. He again emphasized the importance of spiritual matters above physical matters. For the Pharisees the most important matter was physical cleanliness, but in Jesus' view some-one was considered "unclean" by his or her thoughts and words.

---

[207] Eccl.12:14

Matthew 16

"*¹The Pharisees also with the Sadducees came, and tempting desired him that he would shew them a sign from heaven. ² He answered and said unto them, When it is evening, ye say, It will be fair weather: for the sky is red. ³And in the morning, It will be foul weather to day: for the sky is red and lowring. O ye hypocrites, ye can discern the face of the sky; but can ye not discern the signs of the times? ⁴A wicked and adulterous generation seeketh after a sign; and there shall no sign be given unto it, but the sign of the prophet Jonas. And he left them, and departed.*"

The Pharisees and Sadducees usually opposed each other, but here they joined forces to try and trick Jesus by asking him for a sign. Jesus, however, would not make use of his divinity for showmanship or to impress others. He knew that they were prejudiced and full of evil plans. Therefore Jesus reproached them and called them hypocrites. They could study the sky and predict the weather, yet all the signs the prophets foretold regarding the Messiah, were being fulfilled in their time. They were too blind and too self-righteous to see what was happening. Jesus referred them to the sign of Jonah. Jesus would be in the earth for three days and three nights as Jonah was in the belly of a fish. Jonah preached to the people of Nineveh and they repented, unlike the learned Jews who came to Jesus with their unbelieving hearts.[208] Jesus explained in the parable of the rich man and Lazarus in Luke 16:31:

---

[208] Matt.12:40,41

"And he said unto him, If they hear not Moses and the prophets, neither will they be persuaded, though one rose from the dead."

The signs of Jesus being the Messiah were manifested in the miracle healings He performed daily in their midst. He even raised Lazarus from the grave. The Pharisees and Sadducees had no compassion for the sick and down-trodden, but Jesus came to end their suffering, to be a blessing to humanity. He came to show the world the true character of God.

One of the greatest miracles – that of a sinner repenting and finding salvation through the blood of our Redeemer, Jesus Christ, is still being performed daily.

> *"5And when his disciples were come to the other side, they had forgotten to take bread. 6Then Jesus said unto them, Take heed and beware of the leaven of the Pharisees and of the Sadducees. 7And they reasoned among themselves, saying, It is because we have taken no bread. 8Which when Jesus perceived, he said unto them, O ye of little faith, why reason ye among yourselves, because ye have brought no bread? 9Do ye not yet understand, neither remember the five loaves of the five thousand, and how many baskets ye took up? 10Neither the seven loaves of the four thousand, and how many baskets ye took up? 11How is it that ye do not understand that I spake it not to you concerning bread, that ye should beware of the leaven of the Pharisees and of the Sadducees? 12Then understood they how that he bade them not beware of the leaven of bread, but of the doctrine of the Pharisees and of the Sadducees."*

Jesus warned the disciples against the leaven of the Pharisees and the Sadducees.

Again the disciples thought in material terms, while Jesus was referring to the spiritual "leaven". He had to explain to the disciples that he was referring to the shrewd reasoning of the Pharisees and Sadducees. Leaven works invisibly on the dough, but eventually changes its structure. If their false doctrine was accepted, it would make it difficult for people to accept the teachings of Jesus. The Pharisees were people who clung rigidly to their traditions and emphasized their ceremonies and rituals, which included frequent washing, long prayers and the giving of alms. The Sadducees did not believe in the existence of angels or the resurrection of the dead. This topic (the resurrection) frequently caused them to quarrel. The Sadducees also denied the working of the Holy Spirit.

Imbedded in this leaven was the spirit of self-seeking and self-righteousness. Jesus would send the Holy Spirit to help his followers to discern between truth and lies.[209]

> "[13]When Jesus came into the coasts of Caesarea Philippi, he asked his disciples, saying, Whom do men say that I the Son of man am? [14]And they said, Some say that thou art John the Baptist: some, Elias; and others, Jeremias, or one of the prophets. [15]He saith unto them, But whom say ye that I am? [16]And Simon Peter answered and said, Thou art the Christ, the Son of the living God. [17]And Jesus answered and said unto him, Blessed art thou, Simon Barjona: for flesh and blood hath not revealed it unto thee, but my Father which

---

[209] John 16:13,14; John 15:26,27

is in heaven. ¹⁸And I say also unto thee, That thou art Peter, and upon this rock I will build my church; and the gates of hell shall not prevail against it. ¹⁹And I will give unto thee the keys of the kingdom of heaven: and whatsoever thou shalt bind on earth shall be bound in heaven: and whatsoever thou shalt loose on earth shall be loosed in heaven. ²⁰Then charged he his disciples that they should tell no man that he was Jesus the Christ."

Jesus took his disciples aside and asked them who the people said He was. They answered: John the Baptist, Elijah, Jeremiah or one of the prophets. This demonstrated that the majority did not recognize Jesus as the Messiah.

Then He asked them directly: who do you say that I am?

Simon Peter gave the correct answer. Jesus commended him for speaking the truth: that He was the long-awaited Messiah. Faith in Him would be the foundation of the Christian church. It was the Father who revealed this to Peter through the working of the Holy Spirit.

Jesus himself is the Rock upon which the church would be built. He was often referred to as a Rock even in the Old Testament.[210] At that time the church was made up of only a small group of people, but it was built on the Rock. The church would grow into millions of believers. Jesus honored Peter by saying to him that He would give him the keys to the kingdom – these are the words of Holy

---

[210] Deut.32:4; Ps.62:7; Isa.28:16

Scripture. Jesus repeated these words later to all of his disciples (Matt.28:19,20).

> *"²¹From that time forth began Jesus to shew unto his disciples, how that he must go unto Jerusalem, and suffer many things of the elders and chief priests and scribes, and be killed, and be raised again the third day. ²²Then Peter took him, and began to rebuke him, saying, Be it far from thee, Lord: this shall not be unto thee. ²³But he turned, and said unto Peter, Get thee behind me, Satan: thou art an offence unto me: for thou savourest not the things that be of God, but those that be of men."*

The same Peter that just moments before confessed that Jesus was indeed the Messiah, now spoke words of distrust and fallacy, for which he was seriously rebuked. Peter did not want to hear the truth spoken by Jesus of His coming trial en death, and thought that he would prevent it by his own strength. Although he had good intentions, he did not take the words of Jesus seriously and at that time could not understand the mission of Jesus to die for the sins of the world.

> *"²⁴Then said Jesus unto his disciples, If any man will come after me, let him deny himself, and take up his cross, and follow me. ²⁵For whosoever will save his life shall lose it: and whosoever will lose his life for my sake shall find it. ²⁶For what is a man profited, if he shall gain the whole world, and lose his own soul? or what shall a man give in exchange for his soul? ²⁷For the Son of man shall come in the glory of his Father with his angels; and then he shall reward every man according to his works. ²⁸Verily I say unto you, There be some standing here, which shall not taste of death, till they see the Son of man coming in his kingdom."*

The words spoken by Jesus in verses 24 to 27 are clear and to the point and were repeated by Him a few times: following Him is going to be difficult, but in the end every one of His true followers will be rewarded when He comes again. Verse 28 is fulfilled in the next chapter when three of the disciples saw Jesus being glorified.

Matthew 17
"¹And after six days Jesus taketh Peter, James, and John his brother, and bringeth them up into an high mountain apart, ²And was transfigured before them: and his face did shine as the sun, and his raiment was white as the light. ³And, behold, there appeared unto them Moses and Elias talking with him. ⁴Then answered Peter, and said unto Jesus, Lord, it is good for us to be here: if thou wilt, let us make here three tabernacles; one for thee, and one for Moses, and one for Elias. ⁵While he yet spake, behold, a bright cloud overshadowed them: and behold a voice out of the cloud, which said, This is my beloved Son, in whom I am well pleased; hear ye him. ⁶And when the disciples heard it, they fell on their face, and were sore afraid. ⁷And Jesus came and touched them, and said, Arise, and be not afraid. ⁸And when they had lifted up their eyes, they saw no man, save Jesus only. ⁹And as they came down from the mountain, Jesus charged them, saying, Tell the vision to no man, until the Son of man be risen again from the dead."

Jesus took Peter, James and John and led them to a lonely place on a high mountain.

Suddenly God endowed Him with divine glory and the place where He stood shone with brightness. His countenance and clothes shone with a bright holy radiance.

The disciples were awe-struck. They could almost not endure the brightness of His being, but as their eyes grew accustomed to the light, they saw two heavenly beings with Jesus. They were identified as Moses and Elijah who had been taken into heaven. Moses was resurrected when Satan wanted to claim his body[211] and therefore represented the dead who will be resurrected at Christ's second coming. Elijah was translated to heaven, representing those who would be alive at the second coming of Jesus. These people will be changed in an instant.[212] When Jesus returns to the earth for the second time, it will be with all His power and glory, accompanied by all the holy angels.[213]

By this demonstration on the mountain, the disciples were given a prophetic glimpse of Christ's second coming. They could not quite grasp the meaning of this scene at that time, but they were thrilled and amazed to behold their glorified Savior.

Peter wanted this exaltation of Jesus to last, not understanding His mission at the cross. Maybe it was for this reason that Jesus did not want them to speak of the incident, yet.

In hind sight the transfiguration on the mountain would encourage them after Jesus was gone. It

---

[211] Jude 1:9
[212] 1Cor.15:51-53
[213] Hebr.9:28: Mark 8:38

inspired them to look forward to Jesus' second coming. This experience strengthened their faith in Jesus as the Messiah.[214]

When they heard the voice of God saying: *"This is my beloved Son in whom I am well pleased; hear ye him."* the disciples fell flat on the ground, totally awe-struck, until Jesus came over and touched them. Suddenly they were alone again with Jesus. The same words were spoken from heaven, earlier, after the baptism of Jesus:

> *Matt. 3:16: And Jesus, when he was baptized, went up straightway out of the water: and, lo, the heavens were opened unto him, and he saw the Spirit of God descending like a dove, and lighting upon him: 3:17 And lo a voice from heaven, saying, This is my beloved Son, in whom I am well pleased.*

It is interesting to note that when God the Father spoke the second time, He added: *'"hear ye him".*

> *"¹⁰And his disciples asked him, saying, Why then say the scribes that Elias must first come? ¹¹And Jesus answered and said unto them, Elias truly shall first come, and restore all things. ¹²But I say unto you, That Elias is come already, and they knew him not, but have done unto him whatsoever they listed. Likewise shall also the Son of man suffer of them. ¹³Then the disciples understood that he spake unto them of John the Baptist."*

John the Baptist was also not recognized for the prophet he was, bringing the good news of the

---

[214] 2Pet.1:16

coming Kingdom of heaven and the coming of the promised Messiah.[215]

> "*[14]And when they were come to the multitude, there came to him a certain man, kneeling down to him, and saying, [15]Lord, have mercy on my son: for he is lunatick, and sore vexed: for ofttimes he falleth into the fire, and oft into the water. [16]And I brought him to thy disciples, and they could not cure him. [17]Then Jesus answered and said, O faithless and perverse generation, how long shall I be with you? how long shall I suffer you? bring him hither to me. [18]And Jesus rebuked the devil; and he departed out of him: and the child was cured from that very hour.*
> *[19]Then came the disciples to Jesus apart, and said, Why could not we cast him out? [20]And Jesus said unto them, Because of your unbelief: for verily I say unto you, If ye have faith as a grain of mustard seed, ye shall say unto this mountain, Remove hence to yonder place; and it shall remove; and nothing shall be impossible unto you. [21]Howbeit this kind goeth not out but by prayer and fasting.*"

Jesus taught his disciples that their faith should be sincere. They had too much faith in themselves and not enough faith in Jesus.[216] Jesus referred figuratively to mountains as great obstacles that could come their way. For with God nothing is impossible.[217] Sometimes they need to fast and pray in all earnestness before an answer would be given.

> "*[22]And while they abode in Galilee, Jesus said unto them, The Son of man shall be betrayed into the hands of men: [23]And they shall kill*

---

[215] Matt.3:2,14; Mal.3:1; Mal.4:5
[216] Matt.8:26
[217] Matt.19:26

him, and the third day he shall be raised again. And they were exceeding sorry. ²⁴And when they were come to Capernaum, they that received tribute money came to Peter, and said, Doth not your master pay tribute? ²⁵He saith, Yes. And when he was come into the house, Jesus prevented him, saying, What thinkest thou, Simon? of whom do the kings of the earth take custom or tribute? of their own children, or of strangers? ²⁶Peter saith unto him, Of strangers. Jesus saith unto him, Then are the children free. ²⁷Notwithstanding, lest we should offend them, go thou to the sea, and cast an hook, and take up the fish that first cometh up; and when thou hast opened his mouth, thou shalt find a piece of money: that take, and give unto them for me and thee."

Again Jesus foretold them of his coming trial, death and resurrection. It seems as if the disciples then started to believe Jesus and this made them extremely sorrowful.

The official at the temple also tried to trick Jesus by asking the tribute money from Peter. Prophets, priests and Levites in service of the temple, were exempt from paying taxes. Therefore it was actually wrong of Peter to agree to pay the tax. Jesus explained this to Peter, but nevertheless gave him the instruction to catch a fish and give the money inside the fish to the official not to cause trouble. Again Jesus used a miracle to help Peter to believe in His power.

Matthew 18
"¹At the same time came the disciples unto Jesus, saying, Who is the greatest in the kingdom of heaven? ²And Jesus called a little child unto him, and set him in the midst of them, ³And said, Verily I

say unto you, Except ye be converted, and become as little children, ye shall not enter into the kingdom of heaven. ⁴Whosoever therefore shall humble himself as this little child, the same is greatest in the kingdom of heaven. ⁵And whoso shall receive one such little child in my name receiveth me. ⁶But whoso shall offend one of these little ones which believe in me, it were better for him that a millstone were hanged about his neck, and that he were drowned in the depth of the sea."

In this chapter Jesus directs His teaching towards His disciples. He taught them the significance of a humble spirit.

Although Jesus had explained to the disciples in the preceding chapter (Matt.17:22-23) about His upcoming ordeal, they were still concerned about their own rank and position in the new Kingdom. Therefore Jesus could judge by their wrong attitude that they still needed to be converted: they had still to turn away from their old way of thinking and doing. They still had to die to their own selves and fully submit to God. He tried to explain to them the meaning of humility through the example of a little child. Small children naturally display simple trust, confiding love and dependence. Jesus tried to get the truth across that true greatness is not found in riches, fame or position, but in true commitment to Him – putting one's trust in Him and being obedient to His Word. It is pride that keeps many from truly committing themselves to Jesus.

Symbolically, Jesus could also be referring to newly converted Christians who are in need of guidance..." *one of these little ones which believe in me"* and how these ones were to be respected and cared for.[218] In viewing this section as a whole: (Matthew 18: 3-20) – it becomes clear that Jesus' thoughts went from the humility of a small child to the caring of a lost sheep – a person new in the faith, one who temporarily lost track of the truth. Jesus said: woe to someone who causes these little ones to stumble. Jesus had through example and teaching at several occasions stressed that those were seen as inferior beings in the Jewish tradition: women, children, the poor or the sick, were not regarded as inferior by Him and that his followers were to give special regard to those who are most vulnerable.

> "⁷Woe unto the world because of offences! for it must needs be that offences come; but woe to that man by whom the offence cometh!"

The words speak for themselves. It is clear that sin will not be tolerated and those who are the cause of another's downfall (like the symbolical stumbling-block), will be severely punished. It is noted in heaven when a person, by example, words and deliberate attempt, causes others to stumble. Inspired by Satan, some who call themselves Christians will turn people away from Christ. There are those who misrepresent His character and Word. In this way many are being mislead and will miss salvation. Habits and examples leading people to sin bring dishonor to Christ. We are to be living

---

[218] Eph.4:14,15

sacrifices — acceptable to God.[219] Any unrighteousness should be removed from our lives.

> *"⁸Wherefore if thy hand or thy foot offend thee, cut them off, and cast them from thee: it is better for thee to enter into life halt or maimed, rather than having two hands or two feet to be cast into everlasting fire. ⁹And if thine eye offend thee, pluck it out, and cast it from thee: it is better for thee to enter into life with one eye, rather than having two eyes to be cast into hell fire."*

Again Jesus emphasized his teachings of Matt. 5:29, 30 that our spiritual well-being and salvation are more important than our fleshly bodies, using extreme examples to drive home the importance of the matter. We should be aware that our evil habits could mislead others.[220] We could rather loose a hand, a foot or an eye than loose our lives in eternity.

> *"¹⁰Take heed that ye despise not one of these little ones; for I say unto you, That in heaven their angels do always behold the face of my Father which is in heaven."*

In verse 10 Jesus mentions an interesting fact with regard to these little ones: *their* angels make their needs known to the Father in heaven. Jesus confirms thus that children do have guardian angels, looking after their interests and bringing their needs before the Father.

---

[219] Rom.12:1
[220] 1 Cor.8:9; Luke 11:52

> [11] *For the Son of man is come to save that which was lost. [12] How think ye? if a man have an hundred sheep, and one of them be gone astray, doth he not leave the ninety and nine, and goeth into the mountains, and seeketh that which is gone astray? [13] And if so be that he find it, verily I say unto you, he rejoiceth more of that sheep, than of the ninety and nine which went not astray. [14] Even so it is not the will of your Father which is in heaven, that one of these little ones should perish.*

It is important to note that the mission of Jesus was to save the lost.[221] Jesus demonstrated through this parable how the church should care for someone who had gone astray, namely with compassion and special care.[222] Heaven rejoices when one of God's lost children is returned to His fold. It will be to a person's credit if he could help someone return to God.[223] Verse 14 is a very important verse which affirms that God does not want anyone, not even a child, to be lost.

> "[15] *Moreover if thy brother shall trespass against thee, go and tell him his fault between thee and him alone: if he shall hear thee, thou hast gained thy brother. [16] But if he will not hear thee, then take with thee one or two more, that in the mouth of two or three witnesses every word may be established. [17] And if he shall neglect to hear them, tell it unto the church: but if he neglect to hear the church, let him be unto thee as an heathen man and a publican.*"

Jesus taught us in a very direct manner how to deal with someone who had offended us. Firstly go to this person and discuss the matter. If consensus

---

[221] Matt.1:21;Joh.3:16
[222] Gal.6:1,2; Rom.15:1
[223] James 5:20

could not be reached, then take one or two people with you and discuss the matter again. Thereafter the matter should be revealed to the church (the body of local believers). If the person cannot be persuaded of his error, then the matter is closed – nothing more can be done, but to let him leave if that is his will. There should also be a cut-off point where the line is drawn and someone be left to bear the consequences of his own choices and then the church is advised to regard the person as a heathen, that is, they must be evangelized as such and not condemned.[224]

But in view of the parable preceding this judgment – it is not God's will that anybody should be lost.[225] The choice will be theirs.

> "[18]Verily I say unto you, Whatsoever ye shall bind on earth shall be bound in heaven: and whatsoever ye shall loose on earth shall be loosed in heaven.
> [19]Again I say unto you, That if two of you shall agree on earth as touching any thing that they shall ask, it shall be done for them of my Father which is in heaven. [20]For where two or three are gathered together in my name, there am I in the midst of them."

Jesus explained that if people stood together in prayer and faith, He will be their leader and provider. If the decisions taken are in accordance with the principles of God's will, then they are upheld even in heaven.

---

[224] 2 Cor.6:14
[225] 2 Pet.3:9; 1Tim.2:3,4

"²¹Then came Peter to him, and said, Lord, how oft shall my brother sin against me, and I forgive him? till seven times? ²²Jesus saith unto him, I say not unto thee, Until seven times: but, Until seventy times seven. ²³Therefore is the kingdom of heaven likened unto a certain king, which would take account of his servants. ²⁴And when he had begun to reckon, one was brought unto him, which owed him ten thousand talents. ²⁵But forasmuch as he had not to pay, his lord commanded him to be sold, and his wife, and children, and all that he had, and payment to be made. ²⁶The servant therefore fell down, and worshipped him, saying, Lord, have patience with me, and I will pay thee all. ²⁷Then the lord of that servant was moved with compassion, and loosed him, and forgave him the debt. ²⁸But the same servant went out, and found one of his fellowservants, which owed him an hundred pence: and he laid hands on him, and took him by the throat, saying, Pay me that thou owest. ²⁹And his fellowservant fell down at his feet, and besought him, saying, Have patience with me, and I will pay thee all. ³⁰And he would not: but went and cast him into prison, till he should pay the debt. ³¹So when his fellowservants saw what was done, they were very sorry, and came and told unto their lord all that was done. ³²Then his lord, after that he had called him, said unto him, O thou wicked servant, I forgave thee all that debt, because thou desiredst me: ³³Shouldest not thou also have had compassion on thy fellowservant, even as I had pity on thee? ³⁴And his lord was wroth, and delivered him to the tormentors, till he should pay all that was due unto him. ³⁵So likewise shall my heavenly Father do also unto you, if ye from your hearts forgive not every one his brother their trespasses."

It was already mentioned in the Lord's Prayer[226] that forgiveness is a two-way transaction. This is further explained in the preceding parable. It does not make sense that I, who was forgiven my gross iniquities through the blood sacrifice of Jesus Christ,

---

[226] Matt.6:12

should demand from others everything they owe me and thus harbor an unforgiving spirit. We should demonstrate compassion and empathy towards others as the Lord had shown towards us. When we ask for forgiveness we should be aware of how willing we ourselves were to forgive. This goes hand-in-hand with "love your neighbor as yourself".

Peter thought to suggest seven times would be appropriate – as the Pharisees taught to forgive three times. Forgiveness as demonstrated by Jesus was more than the resolution of conflict – it would give the erring one an opportunity to turn away from his wrong doing. Jesus gave a number which would be impossible to count – it is not a matter of counting legally the times someone was forgiven, but having a spirit of forgiveness toward someone repentant.

The debt in the parable represents sin - the man in the parable's sins, like ours, were too much to repay. Jesus set us free from sin by dying in our place on the cross. When we truly repent and accept this free gift, our hearts should be changed in such a manner that we should have compassion with our fellow human beings. Therefore the conduct of the unforgiving servant was unacceptable.

We cannot work or buy our way into heaven – it is a free gift – accepting Jesus' salvation. Our lack of demonstrating our faith through our words or deeds can, however, result in our missing heaven and eternal life. This was demonstrated by Jesus later and recorded in Matthew 25:31-46.

With this parable Jesus again illustrated that wrong deeds sprung from wrong motives, coming forth from twisted minds. Truly converted people are humble and forgiving. They will not even think of counting how many times they had forgiven someone, but will follow the example of Jesus in being compassionate to others.

Matthew 19

"1And it came to pass, that when Jesus had finished these sayings, he departed from Galilee, and came into the coasts of Judea beyond Jordan; 2And great multitudes followed him; and he healed them there.
3The Pharisees also came unto him, tempting him, and saying unto him, Is it lawful for a man to put away his wife for every cause? 4And he answered and said unto them, Have ye not read, that he which made them at the beginning made them male and female, 5And said, For this cause shall a man leave father and mother, and shall cleave to his wife: and they twain shall be one flesh? 6Wherefore they are no more twain, but one flesh. What therefore God hath joined together, let not man put asunder. 7They say unto him, Why did Moses then command to give a writing of divorcement, and to put her away? 8He saith unto them, Moses because of the hardness of your hearts suffered you to put away your wives: but from the beginning it was not so. 9And I say unto you, Whosoever shall put away his wife, except it be for fornication, and shall marry another, committeth adultery: and whoso marrieth her which is put away doth commit adultery. 10His disciples say unto him, If the case of the man be so with his wife, it is not good to marry. 11But he said unto them, All men cannot receive this saying, save they to whom it is given. 12For there are some eunuchs, which were so born from their mother's womb: and there are some eunuchs, which were made

eunuchs of men: and there be eunuchs, which have made themselves eunuchs for the kingdom of heaven's sake. He that is able to receive it, let him receive it."

The Pharisees asked these questions with the purpose to entrap Jesus as they were planning a case against Him. Jesus referred them to the law.[227] At creation the institution of marriage was ordained by God after He created man and woman. The union between a man and his wife should be complete. When this unity is sanctioned by God, it should not be broken. Moses found that people were disloyal and untrustworthy and thus allowed divorce, although this was never God's original intention.[228] Christians should not resort to divorce as a first option to resolve marital problems, but bring the matter before the Lord in prayer. Unfaithful marital partners practicing fornication were stoned under the Law of Moses.[229] The innocent party was free to marry again. Jesus stated that a person who married an illegally divorced woman or man also committed adultery. From this it is clear that divorce should not be an easy solution as it was not in God's original design. We too often choose the easy way out by means of divorce instead of resolving the matter prayerfully.

A eunuch refers to a castrated male, employed in the past in harems or in Oriental courts and under

---

[227] Mark 7:6-8; Isa.29:13,14
[228] Deut.24:1-4
[229] Lev.20:10

the Roman Empire. Jesus evidently referred to a eunuch in the first place as those born with congenital defects. In the second place those who were employed as chamberlains were "made eunuchs".

God created man and woman as Jesus explained in verses 4 to 6 and ordained marriage as a sacred institution. Many disciples were married[230] and nowhere did Jesus tell them to discard their wives. Nor did He indicate that those practicing celibacy will be in a superior position to married men. In 1 Cor.7:29 Paul explained that the time is short and that marriage placed more responsibilities on those who were totally committed to the Lord's work. Jesus probably referred to the same scenario in the latter part of verse 12. Acts of homosexuality was clearly prohibited in the Old Testament, as well as in the New Testament (Rom.1:27-32), and was called an abomination[231].

> "*13Then were there brought unto him little children, that he should put his hands on them, and pray: and the disciples rebuked them. 14But Jesus said, Suffer little children, and forbid them not, to come unto me: for of such is the kingdom of heaven. 15And he laid his hands on them, and departed thence."

Jesus did not appreciate the disciple's effort to spare Him from unnecessary interruptions by keeping the children away from Him. Jesus was not

---

[230] Mark 1:30
[231] Lev.18:22; Lev.20:13

pleased with this attitude at all.[232]Jesus said that they should allow the children to come to Him. He had a special affection for children and they demonstrated an untainted love and devotion for Him. He used them in various illustrations.[233]Parents should not overlook the importance of teaching children about Jesus as they have a special place in God's kingdom.

> "[16]And, behold, one came and said unto him, Good Master, what good thing shall I do, that I may have eternal life? [17]And he said unto him, Why callest thou me good? there is none good but one, that is, God: but if thou wilt enter into life, keep the commandments. [18]He saith unto him, Which? Jesus said, Thou shalt do no murder, Thou shalt not commit adultery, Thou shalt not steal, Thou shalt not bear false witness, [19]Honour thy father and thy mother: and, Thou shalt love thy neighbour as thyself. [20]The young man saith unto him, All these things have I kept from my youth up: what lack I yet? [21]Jesus said unto him, If thou wilt be perfect, go and sell that thou hast, and give to the poor, and thou shalt have treasure in heaven: and come and follow me. [22]But when the young man heard that saying, he went away sorrowful: for he had great possessions.
> [23]Then said Jesus unto his disciples, Verily I say unto you, That a rich man shall hardly enter into the kingdom of heaven. [24]And again I say unto you, It is easier for a camel to go through the eye of a needle, than for a rich man to enter into the kingdom of God. [25]When his disciples heard it, they were exceedingly amazed, saying, Who then can be saved? [26]But Jesus beheld them, and said unto them, With men this is impossible; but with God all things are possible."

Did the rich young man try to flatter Jesus by calling Him good? Probably – and Jesus brought it under

---

[232] Mark 10:14
[233] Matt.11:16,17; Matt.18:3-6

his attention that only God is good – thus if he was sincere with his remarks he would be serious in his encounter with Jesus. It appears, however, that he only wanted to have the security of inheriting eternal life. He found that material riches did not bring happiness and felt that something was lacking in his life. He kept the Ten Commandments in a legalistic way, as he was taught. Important to note that Jesus admonished the young man to keep the Ten Commandments and at no stage did Jesus teach anyone anything otherwise.

Jesus put him to the ultimate test. If he was genuine in his belief that Jesus was God, he would leave everything and follow the Master. But this would result in him moving from a high profile of successful businessman/owner to a low profile student or follower of Jesus. Jesus also told him to sell all his belongings and give it to the poor; to totally surrender his life to Jesus – to wholly commit his life to God. He was not ready to make this move. He could not part with his riches. It gave him security and status. And as Jesus explained: it is hard for a rich person to overcome their self-centeredness, their feeling of self-sufficiency. If they totally submit to God it will be possible to rearrange their priorities. In Jesus' statement: *"With men this is impossible, but with God all things are possible"*, **He was not merely speaking words of comfort to His disciples, but was referring to the role of the Holy Spirit, after Jesus had gone to heaven. The Spirit would move even hardened, selfish hearts.**

This incident illustrated the hold earthly possessions often have on us, standing in the way of our spiritual growth. Our things then own us instead of us owning them. Often preachers will be quick to say that this incident in the Bible does not mean that we all have to sell our belongings and follow Jesus, but it might be exactly what is required of you and me. Nothing should ever stand between us and eternal salvation. To be wholly consecrated to the service of the Lord does not necessitate a full-time job in the ministry, but on the other hand it might mean exactly that. We should be willing and open to go where the Holy Spirit is leading us. Thus with God all things are possible.

> "*27Then answered Peter and said unto him, Behold, we have forsaken all, and followed thee; what shall we have therefore? 28And Jesus said unto them, Verily I say unto you, That ye which have followed me, in the regeneration when the Son of man shall sit in the throne of his glory, ye also shall sit upon twelve thrones, judging the twelve tribes of Israel. 29And every one that hath forsaken houses, or brethren, or sisters, or father, or mother, or wife, or children, or lands, for my name's sake, shall receive an hundredfold, and shall inherit everlasting life. 30But many that are first shall be last; and the last shall be first."*

Peter was starting to feel confident about his own future in God's kingdom, although he completely lacked an understanding of the magnitude thereof. He was encouraged by Jesus, who confirmed that the disciples will have elevated positions in heaven and everybody who gave up all for the sake of Jesus. They will inherit eternal life and all the awesome privileges that it entails.[234] But as a word of warning Jesus added that those who were first, will be last and *vice versa*. It is interesting to note the things that some will have to give up for Jesus: houses, brothers, sisters, father, mother, wife, children or land. This will be a small price to pay in comparison with the riches of everlasting life. Our first priority is to be Jesus Christ, our Savior.

The words of Jesus: *"But many that are first shall be last; and the last shall be first"* (verse 30) must have left some puzzled expressions on the faces of the disciples, so He proceeded to tell the parable that is mentioned in the next chapter to further illustrate the point He was trying to drive home.

The spirit of pride and strife for power displayed by the disciples was the same that brought discord in heaven when Lucifer said: *"I will be like the Most High"*[235] and was cast out of heaven with a third of the angels who followed him in rebellion.

When the Holy Spirit prevails in our hearts there will be no seeking of our own interests, desiring the highest position, but self-sacrificing love will take its place.

Matthew 20
"¹For the kingdom of heaven is like unto a man that is an householder, which went out early in the morning to hire labourers into his vineyard. ²And when he had agreed with the labourers for a

---

[234] Rev.21:1-7
[235] Isa.14:12-14; Eze.28:12-17

penny a day, he sent them into his vineyard. ³And he went out about the third hour, and saw others standing idle in the marketplace, ⁴And said unto them; Go ye also into the vineyard, and whatsoever is right I will give you. And they went their way. ⁵Again he went out about the sixth and ninth hour, and did likewise. ⁶And about the eleventh hour he went out, and found others standing idle, and saith unto them, Why stand ye here all the day idle? ⁷They say unto him, Because no man hath hired us. He saith unto them, Go ye also into the vineyard; and whatsoever is right, that shall ye receive. ⁸So when even was come, the lord of the vineyard saith unto his steward, Call the labourers, and give them their hire, beginning from the last unto the first. ⁹And when they came that were hired about the eleventh hour, they received every man a penny. ¹⁰But when the first came, they supposed that they should have received more; and they likewise received every man a penny. ¹¹And when they had received it, they murmured against the goodman of the house, ¹² Saying, These last have wrought but one hour, and thou hast made them equal unto us, which have borne the burden and heat of the day. ¹³But he answered one of them, and said, Friend, I do thee no wrong: didst not thou agree with me for a penny? ¹⁴Take that thine is, and go thy way: I will give unto this last, even as unto thee. ¹⁵ Is it not lawful for me to do what I will with mine own? Is thine eye evil, because I am good? ¹⁶So the last shall be first, and the first last: for many be called, but few chosen."

Jesus then told another parable to illustrate that His norms differ from those of the world. Those who devote their lives to Jesus Christ will have equal rewards in heaven.

When the man who hired the workers began to pay the workers, he started with those who came last to work. He agreed to pay those who started first a penny, so they expected that they would receive more.

In the world people are paid according to the work done. People expect to be paid what they earn. But in the Kingdom of God things do not operate that way. He says,

"Isa.55:8 For my thoughts [are] not your thoughts, neither [are] your ways my ways, saith the LORD.

55:9 For [as] the heavens are higher than the earth, so are my ways higher than your ways, and my thoughts than your thoughts. "

The owner paid the first laborers what was agreed. God gives His reward according to His own purpose (Titus 3:5).

What matters more to God is the spirit in which the labor was done. Those who came to work at the last hour were grateful to be employed and trusted the employer regarding the reward. They were pleasantly surprised by the employer's generosity. So it is with the sinner whose service to the Lord is short, but he is filled with joy to be accepted by the Lord. We are not saved through our works and God is also not dependent on our works. As is stated in Ephesians:

"2:8 For by grace are ye saved through faith; and that not of yourselves: [it is] the gift of God:

2:9 Not of works, lest any man should boast.

It is when we accept the sacrifice that Jesus made on the cross as remittance for our own sins that we are saved. That is grace. Therefore we have nothing to boast about. Our good works should just be the natural outflow of our love for God.

We should not be focused on the reward, although we should appreciate all the blessings that come from the Lord. Love for God and our fellow human beings should be our motivation and not to receive a reward.

When those who started early complained about their earnings the householder replied,

"Friend, I do thee no wrong: didst not thou agree with me for a penny? ¹⁴Take that thine is, and go thy way: I will give unto this last, even as unto thee. ¹⁵ Is it not lawful for me to do what I will with mine own? Is thine eye evil, because I am good?

This group seemed to forget that God is the Creator and Sustainer of the whole earth and who are we to question Him?

Jesus longs for those who are filled with love and faithfulness. He supports the humble worker who is fully dependent on Him. He sees our faith and no matter how long or how short our service He will reward those who are sincere with eternal life.

In the last sentence of this parable, Jesus explained quite a lot of things. Many are called, but few chosen. Some people will inherit eternal life, despite the fact that they have spent their lives wasted on being caught up in the world and their own egotistical endeavors. On the other hand the chosen are those who heard God's voice and served Him during their life time. This was a special privilege to them – their lives were enriched and their calling gave special meaning to it. It is up to God to reward everyone accordingly. He sensed the underlying competitive spirit amongst the disciples and was trying to correct their erroneous thinking.

Perhaps even today amongst Christians are found feelings of enviousness and competitiveness as to who is more important when in fact, it is the name of God and Jesus Christ that is to be held high. Jesus gave us the example of greatness in service and love for others.[236]

> "*17And Jesus going up to Jerusalem took the twelve disciples apart in the way, and said unto them, 18Behold, we go up to Jerusalem; and the Son of man shall be betrayed unto the chief priests and unto the scribes, and they shall condemn him to death, 19And shall deliver him to the Gentiles to mock, and to scourge, and to crucify him: and the third day he shall rise again.*"

Jesus foretold his coming suffering to the disciples. He knew that He would be crucified. He even told them about his resurrection on the third day. When the events actually took place they did not seem to remember these words, but were overcome with sorrow. Yet it seemed as if they did not grasp the seriousness of the words Jesus spoke in verses 18 and 19, because immediately thereafter another discussion followed, this time by the mother of James and John on where her sons would sit in his kingdom.

> "*20Then came to him the mother of Zebedee's children with her sons, worshipping him, and desiring a certain thing of him. 21And he said unto her, What wilt thou? She saith unto him, Grant that these my*

---

[236] Phil.2:7,8

two sons may sit, the one on thy right hand, and the other on the left, in thy kingdom. ²²But Jesus answered and said, Ye know not what ye ask. Are ye able to drink of the cup that I shall drink of, and to be baptized with the baptism that I am baptized with? They say unto him, We are able. ²³And he saith unto them, Ye shall drink indeed of my cup, and be baptized with the baptism that I am baptized with: but to sit on my right hand, and on my left, is not mine to give, but it shall be given to them for whom it is prepared of my Father."

How ignorant were the disciples of Jesus. They had not yet suffered anything for God's kingdom, nor had they even lived through the crucifixion experience with Jesus, but they wanted to be acknowledged and rewarded. Little did they know what hardship would come their way in standing by Jesus and living for Him. The disciples' understanding was still lacking. They could not see that there would still be a long time ahead in the future in which the Christian church would be established and the message of Jesus be preached to all the corners of the earth. Their characters would have to be strengthened through trials like gold refined in the fire.[237] It is possible to stand for Jesus even when times are difficult, because He will give us the power of the Holy Spirit. When our motives are wrong and we are self-centered we might be mislead to think that we will inherit eternal life, while Jesus does not even know us.[238]

---

[237] Job 23:10; Rev.3:18; Mal.3:3
[238] Matt.7:21-23

"24And when the ten heard it, they were moved with indignation against the two brethren. 25But Jesus called them unto him, and said, Ye know that the princes of the Gentiles exercise dominion over them, and they that are great exercise authority upon them. 26But it shall not be so among you: but whosoever will be great among you, let him be your minister; 27And whosoever will be chief among you, let him be your servant: 28Even as the Son of man came not to be ministered unto, but to minister, and to give his life a ransom for many."

The other disciples got upset with the mother of the two sons of Zebedee. Jesus explained to them that they should not think like the people in the world with their obsession with power. In his kingdom it is more important to serve and to minister to others, than to look important and think of yourself as above others. Jesus spent most of his time serving others.

Matthew 21
"18Now in the morning as he returned into the city, he hungered. 19And when he saw a fig tree in the way, he came to it, and found nothing thereon, but leaves only, and said unto it, Let no fruit grow on thee henceforward for ever. And presently the fig tree withered away. 20And when the disciples saw it, they marvelled, saying, How soon is the fig tree withered away! 21Jesus answered and said unto them, Verily I say unto you, If ye have faith, and doubt not, ye shall not only do this which is done to the fig tree, but also if ye shall say unto this mountain, Be thou removed, and be thou cast into the sea; it shall be done. 22And all things, whatsoever ye shall ask in prayer, believing, ye shall receive."

Jesus used the example of the fig tree to act out a parable. The fig tree was full of leaves and from this tree, fruit could have been expected, yet there was none. Although this was a demonstration of the power of faith, Jesus also demonstrated his hunger to find fruit among the people of Israel and his disappointment when He found none. In their reluctance to demonstrate their knowledge of Scripture and the love of God to others, they had failed to bear fruit and the results were disastrous.[239] In verse 22 we are promised that God listens to our sincere prayers and will put his divine power into action if it is according to his will. The act of Jesus to curse the fig tree was deemed very strange by his disciples as thus far his mission was to heal and to restore.[240] The illustration was used by Jesus to bring to the disciples' attention that judgment would come to those who bear no fruit as was explained by him in the two parables He told following this incident. Although God has no pleasure in the death of the wicked[241] everyone will ultimately be known and judged according to their actions. [242]

> *"23And when he was come into the temple, the chief priests and the elders of the people came unto him as he was teaching, and said, By what authority doest thou these things? and who gave thee this authority? 24And Jesus answered and said unto them, I also will ask you one thing, which if ye tell me, I in like wise will tell you by what authority I do these things. 25The baptism of John, whence was it? from heaven, or of men? And they reasoned with themselves, saying, If we shall say, From heaven; he will say unto us, Why did ye*

---

[239] Matt.21:19
[240] Luke 9:56
[241] Mic.7:18; Eze.33:11
[242] Matt.25:45,46

not then believe him? ²⁶But if we shall say, Of men; we fear the people; for all hold John as a prophet. ²⁷And they answered Jesus, and said, We cannot tell. And he said unto them, Neither tell I you by what authority I do these things."

Jesus knew how to catch people in their own trap. No matter how clever they thought themselves to be, they could not outsmart Him. He told the following parable to illustrate the reluctance that existed among the high-ranking Jews to accept the truth that was offered to them and to act upon it.

"²⁸But what think ye? A certain man had two sons; and he came to the first, and said, Son, go work to day in my vineyard. ²⁹He answered and said, I will not: but afterward he repented, and went. ³⁰And he came to the second, and said likewise. And he answered and said, I go, sir: and went not. ³¹Whether of them twain did the will of his father? They say unto him, The first. Jesus saith unto them, Verily I say unto you, That the publicans and the harlots go into the kingdom of God before you. ³²For John came unto you in the way of righteousness, and ye believed him not: but the publicans and the harlots believed him: and ye, when ye had seen it, repented not afterward, that ye might believe him."

Jesus used John as an example of how readily the common people accepted the truth of his message, yet most of the learned and important people of the time rejected him. And even in hind sight they did not repent. Jesus followed up with another parable to state His case even clearer.

"³³Hear another parable: There was a certain householder, which planted a vineyard, and hedged it round about, and digged a winepress in it, and built a tower, and let it out to husbandmen, and went into a far country: ³⁴And when the time of the fruit drew near,

he sent his servants to the husbandmen, that they might receive the fruits of it. ³⁵And the husbandmen took his servants, and beat one, and killed another, and stoned another. ³⁶Again, he sent other servants more than the first: and they did unto them likewise. ³⁷But last of all he sent unto them his son, saying, They will reverence my son. ³⁸But when the husbandmen saw the son, they said among themselves, This is the heir; come, let us kill him, and let us seize on his inheritance. ³⁹And they caught him, and cast him out of the vineyard, and slew him. ⁴⁰When the lord therefore of the vineyard cometh, what will he do unto those husbandmen? ⁴¹They say unto him, He will miserably destroy those wicked men, and will let out his vineyard unto other husbandmen, which shall render him the fruits in their seasons."

To Israel were sent many prophets (servants) to foretell of the coming of the Messiah[243] and eventually God sent His own Son, but instead of changing their wrong course, they killed Him. The knowledge of Scripture that they had to witness to those around them, they did not use. They made their own rules and changed God's Word into rituals, placing heavy burdens on people with their man-made traditions. Instead of living out the core message of the law of love for God and fellow human beings, they concentrated on their national pride.[244] Instead of realizing what a wonderful privilege God had bestowed upon Israel to personally witness the coming of the Messiah, they had rejected Him, as well as the prophets that came to foretell His coming. A certain time was set aside

---

[243] Ps.22:28,29; Isa.53:1-13; Isa.61:1; Zech.12:10; Jer.33:14-16; Dan.7:13,14
[244] Hos.13:9; Jer.6:19

to bring the message of salvation to Israel. Thereafter it would go to the whole world. Jesus already knew the way He was going to die and who would be responsible for killing Him (Dan.9:24-27).

> "42 *Jesus saith unto them, Did ye never read in the scriptures, The stone which the builders rejected, the same is become the head of the corner: this is the Lord's doing, and it is marvellous in our eyes?* 43*Therefore say I unto you, The kingdom of God shall be taken from you, and given to a nation bringing forth the fruits thereof.* 44*And whosoever shall fall on this stone shall be broken: but on whomsoever it shall fall, it will grind him to powder.* 45*And when the chief priests and Pharisees had heard his parables, they perceived that he spake of them.* 46*But when they sought to lay hands on him, they feared the multitude, because they took him for a prophet."*

Most of the Jews rejected the Rock of Ages who was the cornerstone of the Christian church. The stone (Rock) will put you before the ultimate choice: fall on the Rock (in humility accept Him as your Lord and Savior)[245] or the Rock will fall on you and grind you to powder.[246] He will ultimately judge those who rejected Him.

It is interesting to note that the chief priest and Pharisees immediately understood that Jesus was referring to them in this parable. Even so, as Jesus stated in the previous parable, it is mind-boggling that they persisted in their course to kill Him and not to accept Him as the promised Messiah.[247]

---

[245] Ps. 34:18; Ps 51:17
[246] Mal.4:3
[247] Isa.53

Matthew 22 *"¹And Jesus answered and spake unto them again by parables, and said, ²The kingdom of heaven is like unto a certain king, which made a marriage for his son, ³And sent forth his servants to call them that were bidden to the wedding: and they would not come. ⁴Again, he sent forth other servants, saying, Tell them which are bidden, Behold, I have prepared my dinner: my oxen and my fatlings are killed, and all things are ready: come unto the marriage. ⁵But they made light of it, and went their ways, one to his farm, another to his merchandise: ⁶And the remnant took his servants, and entreated them spitefully, and slew them. ⁷But when the king heard thereof, he was wroth: and he sent forth his armies, and destroyed those murderers, and burned up their city. ⁸Then saith he to his servants, The wedding is ready, but they which were bidden were not worthy. ⁹Go ye therefore into the highways, and as many as ye shall find, bid to the marriage. ¹⁰So those servants went out into the highways, and gathered together all as many as they found, both bad and good: and the wedding was furnished with guests. ¹¹And when the king came in to see the guests, he saw there a man which had not on a wedding garment: ¹²And he saith unto him, Friend, how camest thou in hither not having a wedding garment? And he was speechless. ¹³Then said the king to the servants, Bind him hand and foot, and take him away, and cast him into outer darkness; there shall be weeping and gnashing of teeth. ¹⁴For many are called, but few are chosen."*

This parable in Matthew 22 is a continuation of the teaching of Jesus in Matthew 21. Many of the parables told by Jesus had the recurring theme; The Father sends his servants to invite people to a feast/wedding of his son. The invitees do not respond favorably (in a variation of ways); they have to face the consequences of their choice.

For many are called, but few *are* chosen: this is one of Jesus' famous quotes, because it is one of those phrases He repeated on several occasions. It is a loaded statement. In the context of the above parable a person had to take two steps: firstly to accept the invitation to attend the wedding feast, and secondly to be clothed by the garment provided by the King. Those who ignored the invitation do not seem to understand the power and authority of the King. They are not even aware, it seems, that there will be dire consequences for them in ignoring His friendly invitation.

Many people want to be in heaven and have eternal life, but they forget that we need to be covered by the righteousness of Jesus Christ. It seems as if the guest who came to the wedding without wearing the right garment, was interested in going to the feast for the obvious benefit. He did not however, be closely connected to the King by wearing this garment provided for his guests. We can only be saved when we accept salvation through Jesus Christ as He died on the cross for you and me. That is when we wear his cloak of righteousness.

The explanation in all these related parables remained basically the same, namely:

TABLE 6   EXPLANATION OF PARABLE

A king	God the Father
Prepared a wedding	Important, joyous occasion of God trying to unite/fellowship with his people
for his son	Jesus Christ
He sent his servants – more	Prophets/ John the Baptist/

than once	the disciples
To invite (by the time the servants went out, those "bidden" already knew they were invited)	Giving them a free choice – a friendly reminder
The invitees ignore the invitation	Many Jews who knew the message of the Old Testament prophets ignored the coming of the Messiah and his message[248]
The feast is ready – everything is prepared	The Messiah has come and the time is ready
The invitees turn nasty	They not only ignore the messengers but kill them
The King gets angry and destroys them and their city	The reference to their city, Jerusalem, was a foreboding of the fall of that city in A.D. 70 at the hand of the Romans
The King tells his servants to invite others to wedding	The Gentiles
Go to the highways	The main stream of people from all nations
Invite good and bad – they should not try do discern who to invite	Some had good motives and others bad
The King spots someone without a wedding garment – this was usually provided by the King himself	Someone tried to sneak in on his own merits – not covered by the garment provided by the King himself – he has no excuse
He is taken away and punished	Without the cloak of righteousness of Jesus Christ

---

[248] Isa.53:3; Matt.23:37

	(covered by His blood) we cannot be saved

> "¹⁵Then went the Pharisees, and took counsel how they might entangle him in his talk. ¹⁶And they sent out unto him their disciples with the Herodians, saying, Master, we know that thou art true, and teachest the way of God in truth, neither carest thou for any man: for thou regardest not the person of men. ¹⁷Tell us therefore, What thinkest thou? Is it lawful to give tribute unto Caesar, or not? ¹⁸But Jesus perceived their wickedness, and said, Why tempt ye me, ye hypocrites? ¹⁹Shew me the tribute money. And they brought unto him a penny. ²⁰And he saith unto them, Whose is this image and superscription? ²¹They say unto him, Caesar's. Then saith he unto them, Render therefore unto Caesar the things which are Caesar's; and unto God the things that are God's. ²²When they had heard these words, they marvelled, and left him, and went their way."

This section dealt with questions directed at Jesus by different parties with the aim to "entangle" Him and to acquire evidence against Him.

Even though the Pharisees and the Herodians tried to flatter Jesus, He saw right through them and gave them an answer that caught them completely off-guard. Within the context of these Jew's resentment of the Roman power reigning over them, they asked if it was lawful to pay taxes to Caesar. Jesus' answer was so simple it must have completely baffled them.

> "²³The same day came to him the Sadducees, which say that there is no resurrection, and asked him, ²⁴Saying, Master, Moses said, If a man die, having no children, his brother shall marry his wife, and raise up seed unto his brother. ²⁵Now there were with us seven brethren: and the first, when he had married a wife, deceased, and,

having no issue, left his wife unto his brother: ²⁶Likewise the second also, and the third, unto the seventh. ²⁷And last of all the woman died also. ²⁸Therefore in the resurrection whose wife shall she be of the seven? for they all had her. ²⁹Jesus answered and said unto them, Ye do err, not knowing the scriptures, nor the power of God. ³⁰For in the resurrection they neither marry, nor are given in marriage, but are as the angels of God in heaven. ³¹But as touching the resurrection of the dead, have ye not read that which was spoken unto you by God, saying, ³²I am the God of Abraham, and the God of Isaac, and the God of Jacob? God is not the God of the dead, but of the living. ³³And when the multitude heard this, they were astonished at his doctrine."

The next group that came with a trick question was the Sadducees. They asked the question with regard to a woman who was married to several brothers and their position after resurrection. They themselves did not believe in the resurrection after death and thought they would corner Jesus with this trick question. Jesus set them straight and in so doing brought light to the subject, namely:

- There would be a resurrection of the dead. This was again proven in the account of Jesus' resurrection of Lazarus, the brother of Mary and Martha in John 11:11-26. In this portion of Scripture Jesus said to his disciples that Lazarus was sleeping – but clarified that He meant that Lazarus was dead (verse 14). Martha had the right belief about the resurrection and declared in Joh.11:23-26:

    "²³ Jesus saith unto her, Thy brother shall rise again. ²⁴ Martha saith unto him, I know that he shall rise again in the resurrection at the last

day. ²⁵ Jesus said unto her, I am the resurrection, and the life: he that believeth in me, though he were dead, yet shall he live:"

- The resurrected ones would no longer be sexual beings, but will resemble angels.[249]
- They were wrong in their thinking and they underestimated the divine power of God.
- They did not know Scripture.[250]

Jesus tried to set their corrupt thinking straight. God is the Creator of everything. They were caught up in group thinking – working out a doctrine to suit themselves. God sees the beginning from the end and thus spoke of Abraham, Isaac and Jacob as if they would be alive – which they will be after the resurrection of the righteous at His second coming.[251]

> *"³⁴But when the Pharisees had heard that he had put the Sadducees to silence, they were gathered together. ³⁵Then one of them, which was a lawyer, asked him a question, tempting him, and saying, ³⁶Master, which is the great commandment in the law? ³⁷ Jesus said unto him, Thou shalt love the Lord thy God with all thy heart, and with all thy soul, and with all thy mind. ³⁸This is the first and great commandment. ³⁹And the second is like unto it, Thou shalt love thy neighbour as thyself. ⁴⁰On these two commandments hang all the law and the prophets."*

In the next instance a learned lawyer thought he would eventually trip Jesus up with a question about the most important commandment. The answer

---

[249] 1 Joh.3:2
[250] Ps.16:10
[251] Ex.3:6; 1 Thes.4:13-18; Joh.11:23,24

Jesus gave was a beautiful synopsis of the law. Both aspects of the law stand on the principle of love. The love of God is summed up in the first four commandments.[252] The last six deal with love for our fellow-human beings.[253] When our love for God is in place, the second will follow automatically.[254] This was also summarized in the Old Testament.[255]

Jesus presented the essence of the law as a unit – the underlying principle being that of love. Our love for God will be expressed in our obedience towards all of His commandments.[256]

The scribe who asked Jesus this question was astonished at His insight – he could do nothing but acknowledge that Jesus spoke the truth.

> *"[41]While the Pharisees were gathered together, Jesus asked them, [42]Saying, What think ye of Christ? whose son is he? They say unto him, The Son of David. [43]He saith unto them, How then doth David in spirit call him Lord, saying, [44]The LORD said unto my Lord, Sit thou on my right hand, till I make thine enemies thy footstool? [45]If David then call him Lord, how is he his son? [46]And no man was able to answer him a word, neither durst any man from that day forth ask him any more questions."*

Jesus then turned to the Pharisees and asked them about the Messiah. They answered that He was the Son of David.[257] Many who were healed by Jesus

---

[252] Ex.20:3-11
[253] Ex.20:12-17
[254] 1Joh.2:9; 1Joh.4:7,20
[255] Deut.6:5
[256] 1 Joh.2:3,4

acknowledged him by that title.[258] They could not answer Jesus' question and realized that they could not trip Him up by their craftiness. The right answer would have been: He is the Son of God – the Messiah - but they would not acknowledge this. David was less than Jesus Christ although according to His genealogy He was also the son of David.[259] They must have realized that the status of Jesus grew with the surrounding crowd as he answered them in such a wise and precise way. Therefore they turned away and did not ask him any more questions, but rather plotted to have him killed.

---

[257] Jer.23:5,6
[258] Matt.12:23; 15:22; 21:9,15
[259] Matt.1:1-17

Chapter 5

Comments on the Scribes and Pharisees

Matthew 23
"¹Then spake Jesus to the multitude, and to his disciples, ²Saying, The scribes and the Pharisees sit in Moses' seat: ³All therefore whatsoever they bid you observe, that observe and do; but do not ye after their works: for they say, and do not. ⁴For they bind heavy burdens and grievous to be borne, and lay them on men's shoulders; but they themselves will not move them with one of their fingers. ⁵But all their works they do for to be seen of men: they make broad their phylacteries, and enlarge the borders of their garments, ⁶And love the uppermost rooms at feasts, and the chief seats in the synagogues, ⁷And greetings in the markets, and to be called of men, Rabbi, Rabbi. ⁸But be not ye called Rabbi: for one is your Master, even Christ; and all ye are brethren. ⁹And call no man your father upon the earth: for one is your Father, which is in heaven. ¹⁰Neither be ye called masters: for one is your Master, even Christ. ¹¹But he that is greatest among you shall be your servant. ¹²And whosoever shall exalt himself shall be abased; and he that shall humble himself shall be exalted. "

In the first twelve verses of this chapter Jesus spoke to the disciples and the crowd about the scribes and Pharisees. In the following section He addressed them personally. This was during the last days of Jesus' teaching in the temple. Jesus spoke the unflinching truth with dignity. He revealed to the crowd the corruptness of their leaders – their hypocrisy in teaching one thing, but doing another.

He gave them a warning of the retribution that was sure to follow their evil ways. The priests and elders were exposed before the people and this made them very uneasy. No one had ever dared before to address them like this in front of the people. For the first time the ordinary people saw their religious leaders in a totally different light. They were confused because they were loyal to these pious leaders in the past, yet Jesus clearly acted on their behalf through his caring and healing of the sick. They could not understand the animosity between Jesus and their religious leaders.

Jesus spoke in parables in the past and many could not follow his message. At this instance He spoke outright and revealed the evil ways of these religious groups. Jesus told his hearers that it was the correct thing to do to obey the Law of Moses,[260] as the scribes and Pharisees were supposed to do,[261] but not to follow the example they set. He explained how the way they acted in public was just to look important. They also taught traditional laws that were not found in Scripture, just to impose their power on the people - things they exempted themselves of or secretly did not keep. Their main aim was to attract attention and to look pious in front of the people.

Jesus also condemned the use of titles such as Rabbi, Master and Father. These titles belonged to

---

[260] Ex.20:1-17; Deut.5:6-21
[261] Ezra 7:10

God. God's children are all equal as brothers and sisters in Christ. Jesus taught in verse 11: *"But he that is greatest among you shall be your servant"* If people want to be great in God's estimation, they should serve others through the genuine concern of their compassionate hearts. Jesus emphasized works of love and mercy as He demonstrated throughout His mission on earth.

> *"13But woe unto you, scribes and Pharisees, hypocrites! for ye shut up the kingdom of heaven against men: for ye neither go in yourselves, neither suffer ye them that are entering to go in. 14Woe unto you, scribes and Pharisees, hypocrites! for ye devour widows' houses, and for a pretence make long prayer: therefore ye shall receive the greater damnation. 15Woe unto you, scribes and Pharisees, hypocrites! for ye compass sea and land to make one proselyte, and when he is made, ye make him twofold more the child of hell than yourselves."*

Jesus spoke several woes: exclamations of denunciation - to illustrate the condition of the scribes and Pharisees. See the summary at the end of verse 33 of the things they did which were condemned by Jesus.

> *"16Woe unto you, ye blind guides, which say, Whosoever shall swear by the temple, it is nothing; but whosoever shall swear by the gold of the temple, he is a debtor! 17Ye fools and blind: for whether is greater, the gold, or the temple that sanctifieth the gold? 18And, Whosoever shall swear by the altar, it is nothing; but whosoever sweareth by the gift that is upon it, he is guilty. 19Ye fools and blind: for whether is greater, the gift, or the altar that sanctifieth the gift? 20Whoso therefore shall swear by the altar, sweareth by it, and by all things thereon. 21And whoso shall swear by the temple, sweareth by*

it, and by him that dwelleth therein. ²²And he that shall swear by heaven, sweareth by the throne of God, and by him that sitteth thereon. ²³Woe unto you, scribes and Pharisees, hypocrites! for ye pay tithe of mint and anise and cummin, and have omitted the weightier matters of the law, judgment, mercy, and faith: these ought ye to have done, and not to leave the other undone. ²⁴Ye blind guides, which strain at a gnat, and swallow a camel. ²⁵Woe unto you, scribes and Pharisees, hypocrites! for ye make clean the outside of the cup and of the platter, but within they are full of extortion and excess. ²⁶Thou blind Pharisee, cleanse first that which is within the cup and platter, that the outside of them may be clean also. ²⁷Woe unto you, scribes and Pharisees, hypocrites! for ye are like unto whited sepulchres, which indeed appear beautiful outward, but are within full of dead men's bones, and of all uncleanness. ²⁸Even so ye also outwardly appear righteous unto men, but within ye are full of hypocrisy and iniquity. ²⁹Woe unto you, scribes and Pharisees, hypocrites! because ye build the tombs of the prophets, and garnish the sepulchres of the righteous, ³⁰And say, If we had been in the days of our fathers, we would not have been partakers with them in the blood of the prophets. ³¹Wherefore ye be witnesses unto yourselves, that ye are the children of them which killed the prophets. ³²Fill ye up then the measure of your fathers. ³³Ye serpents, ye generation of vipers, how can ye escape the damnation of hell? "

In summary Jesus held the following acts and attitudes of the scribes and Pharisees against them:

- They prevented others from finding the kingdom of heaven by perverting the Scriptures. Even though they made a great effort to make proselytes (convert people to the Jewish religion), they were leading people astray. They corrupted the thinking of their scholars.

- They influenced pious widows to bequest their property to the temple for religious purposes and through schemes used it to their own benefit.
- They tried to impress others by offering long prayers in public.
- They devised their own system of guilt, e.g. by stating that swearing by the gold of the temple would be more binding than swearing by the temple. They seemed to forget that it was the temple and the altar that were holy[262] and not the gold. Jesus called them blind guides and condemned their spiritual blindness as He tried to show them their ridiculous way of reasoning. A clear instruction was given during the Sermon on the Mount[263]: do not swear at all, i.e. solemn statements to confirm the truth. What Jesus was referring to here was perjury in which the Jews often partook.
- The Jewish leaders conspicuously observed the paying of tithes, while they neglected other more humane duties. Jesus did not say that they should not pay tithes as this was instituted in Scripture[264], but He had it against them that they overlooked other important matters such as **justice, mercy and faith**.
- While they were putting great emphasis on minute details, they completely missed the point

---

[262] Ex.30:26-29
[263] Matt.5:33-37
[264] Mal.3:8-10

of the Law, which is love.[265] The same idea was repeated in verse 24 which referred to their habit to strain water through a cloth to make sure they do not swallow an unclean thing – strain a gnat, but swallow a camel! – they were too blind to see the obvious. They completely missed the essence of the Law. These people are much like those who go through the Bible to find the smallest spelling mistake or little error, but they overlook its main message of salvation and hope of eternal life, so often repeated from Genesis to Revelation. They also strain the gnat but swallow the camel!

- They appeared to be something on the outside which they were not on the inside. Their motives were corrupt.
- They were like white grave stones which appeared to be pure, but were filthy underneath.
- They condemned their forefathers for killing the prophets, while they were planning to kill the Son of God. They were in other words acknowledging that they were partakers in the killing of the prophets. They would also be guilty of the murder of Jesus. Therefore they were condemned by Jesus for final destruction. (See verse 33)

---

[265] Deut.6:5; Matt.22:37-40

TABLE 7 BASIS FOR CONDEMNATION OF SCRIBES AND PHARISEES

Woe 1: verse 13	Mislead others
Woe 2: verse 14	Cheat widows
Woe 3: verse 15	False teaching
Woe 4: verse 16	Perjury
Woe 5: verse 23	Omit judgment, mercy & faith
Woe 6: verse 25	Hypocrisy
Woe 7: verse 27	Full of filth
Woe 8: verse 29	Kill prophets

"*[34]Wherefore, behold, I send unto you prophets, and wise men, and scribes: and some of them ye shall kill and crucify; and some of them shall ye scourge in your synagogues, and persecute them from city to city: [35]That upon you may come all the righteous blood shed upon the earth, from the blood of righteous Abel unto the blood of Zacharias son of Barachias, whom ye slew between the temple and the altar. [36]Verily I say unto you, All these things shall come upon this generation. [37]O Jerusalem, Jerusalem, thou that killest the prophets, and stonest them which are sent unto thee, how often would I have gathered thy children together, even as a hen gathereth her chickens under her wings, and ye would not! [38]Behold, your house is left unto you desolate. [39]For I say unto you, Ye shall not see me henceforth, till ye shall say, Blessed is he that cometh in the name of the Lord.*"

After Jesus had gone, He would send more prophets and wise men and scribes (e.g. Paul) and He knew that these people would be ridiculed and tortured and killed, but that eventually, at the end of time, God will judge everyone that was operational in the murder of His messengers.

Jesus' voice was full of melancholy when He lamented over Jerusalem and its inhabitants and their lack of repentance after decades of warnings. This was Jesus' last fare-well greeting to the city. His prophetic words: *"Behold, your house is left unto you desolate"*[266] refers to the fact that God would no longer be present in the Holy of Holies[267] of the temple. It is significant that Jesus always referred to the temple as "my house", but now He called it "your house".

When Jesus breathed out His last breath, the curtain was torn in two[268] – leaving that area exposed and void. The words of Jesus would further be fulfilled forty years later when Jerusalem and the temple were totally destroyed by a persecuting power (the Romans).[269] This demolition would also help the first Christians to separate their worship from the Jerusalem temple.

Jesus put this catastrophe in the future and thus He was not referring to a disruption in the temple service for three years after Jerusalem was conquered by Antiochus Epiphanies in around 167-164 B.C.

---

[266] Jer.12:7-11; Lam.4:1,13; 5:18; Dan.11:31
[267] Ex.26:33, 34; 2 Chron.3:14;
[268] Matt.27:51
[269] Jer.13:24-27; 2 Chron.24:20,21

God's presence was withdrawn from the temple as Jesus died on the cross, thus demonstrated by the renting of the temple veil. From then on all ceremonies carried out in the temple would be meaningless, as the Lamb of God was sacrificed on the cross.[270] All lambs sacrificed in the past were symbolic of the Lamb that would be slain as sacrifice for the sins of mankind. The curtain that was torn signifying that the presence of God was no longer in the temple also reminded the disciples of Jesus' words that He would rebuild the temple in three days – referring to Himself being raised three days after His crucifixion (John 2:19). The temple was no longer a symbolic part of the people's daily worship as they could approach Him directly through prayer. It would be the central turning point of all history. Everything before that time pointed to the cross and everything after the cross would take place in its shadow.

---

[270] Dan.9:12, 24-27

Chapter 6
Predicting the future

Matthew 24
"¹And Jesus went out, and departed from the temple: and his disciples came to him for to shew him the buildings of the temple. ²And Jesus said unto them, See ye not all these things? verily I say unto you, There shall not be left here one stone upon another, that shall not be thrown down. ³And as he sat upon the mount of Olives, the disciples came unto him privately, saying, Tell us, when shall these things be? and what shall be the sign of thy coming, and of the end of the world?"

In Chapter 24 verse 2 Jesus continued His predictions regarding the destruction of the temple. When the disciples asked Him about the time that those predictions would take place, they did not understand that the destruction of Jerusalem and the temple would not take place simultaneously with Jesus' second coming and the end of the world. It is clear that in verse 2 He was referring to the destruction of the temple in 70 AD.

It seems as if Jesus mixed the two events on purpose in order for them not to leave anything out of what He told them. If He purposefully separated the two events, they probably would not have given as much attention to the event that was still afar off. In the way that He gave it to them, it kept them on their toes (so to speak) and kept their eyes open to what was happening in their world. In hind sight it is easier for us today to ascertain when He was referring to which event, although circumstances before the fall of Jerusalem would be repeated on an ever grander scale at the end of time.

Taken into account that Jesus gave several warnings that His second coming would happen unexpectedly, it was and still is good advice for His followers to be always ready and prepared for this event.

"4And Jesus answered and said unto them, Take heed that no man deceive you. 5For many shall come in my name, saying, I am Christ; and shall deceive many. 6And ye shall hear of wars and rumours of wars: see that ye be not troubled: for all these things must come to pass, but the end is not yet. 7For nation shall rise against nation, and kingdom against kingdom: and there shall be famines, and pestilences, and earthquakes, in divers places. 8All these are the beginning of sorrows. 9Then shall they deliver you up to be afflicted, and shall kill you: and ye shall be hated of all nations for my name's sake. 10And then shall many be offended, and shall betray one another, and shall hate one another. 11And many false prophets shall rise, and shall deceive many. 12And because iniquity shall abound, the love of many shall wax cold. 13But he that shall endure unto the end, the same shall be saved. 14And this gospel of the kingdom shall be preached in all the world for a witness unto all nations; and then shall the end come. 15When ye therefore shall see the abomination of desolation, spoken of by Daniel the prophet, stand in the holy place, (whoso readeth, let him understand:)"

What were the signs the disciples had to be on the look-out for, firstly for the destruction of Jerusalem and secondly for the end of the world? (table 8)

TABLE 8 SIGNS TO LOOK OUT FOR: THE DESTRUCTION OF JERUSALEM AND THE END OF THE WORLD

Signs to watch out for	Referring to which event: the fall of Jerusalem or Jesus' second coming?
Deceivers will appear and pretend to be Christ	Both events
Wars and rumors of wars	Both events
Famines Pestilences Earthquakes – divers places – beginning of sorrows	Increasing in number toward end of the world
Christians shall be delivered, hated & killed	Both events
People shall be offended, betray each other and hate each other	Both events[271]
False prophets will deceive many	Both events and very relevant towards the end of time[272]
Iniquity shall abound	Both, but increasingly toward end of time
Love of many grow cold	Both, but increasingly toward end of time[273]
The Gospel of the kingdom will be preached to all the world as a witness unto all nations	Both events but especially at the end time

---

[271] Matt.10:34-39
[272] 1 Tim.4:1
[273] 2 Tim.3:1-5

see the abomination of desolation, spoken of by Daniel the prophet[274], stand in the holy place	Fall of Jerusalem, God's presence left temple at Jesus' crucifixion – when the temple hanging was torn - thus it was void of God's presence, resulting in spiritual desolation.

"[16]Then let them which be in Judea flee into the mountains: [17]Let him which is on the housetop not come down to take any thing out of his house: [18] Neither let him which is in the field return back to take his clothes. [19]And woe unto them that are with child, and to them that give suck in those days! [20]But pray ye that your flight be not in the winter, neither on the sabbath day."

From verse 16 to verse 20 Jesus gave a very direct warning regarding the time before the destruction of Jerusalem. The Christians were to look out for a time when armies were planning to surround Jerusalem and leave the place immediately. It is interesting to note that Jesus referred to the Sabbath day in verse 20 which affirmed the fact that He did not do away with the Sabbath after his resurrection. No other day of the week except the seventh was ever known as the Sabbath. His followers might be distracted on the Sabbath – busy with the studying of Scripture and not be ready to flee, if these things happened on the Sabbath Day, so they were to pray that it would not fall on the Sabbath. This was also an indication that events would take place rapidly.

---

[274] Dan.11:31

"²¹For then shall be great tribulation, such as was not since the beginning of the world to this time, no, nor ever shall be. ²²And except those days should be shortened, there should no flesh be saved: but for the elect's sake those days shall be shortened.²³Then if any man shall say unto you, Lo, here is Christ, or there; believe it not. ²⁴For there shall arise false Christs, and false prophets, and shall shew great signs and wonders; insomuch that, if it were possible, they shall deceive the very elect. ²⁵Behold, I have told you before. ²⁶Wherefore if they shall say unto you, Behold, he is in the desert; go not forth: behold, he is in the secret chambers; believe it not. ²⁷For as the lightning cometh out of the east, and shineth even unto the west; so shall also the coming of the Son of man be. ²⁸For wheresoever the carcase is, there will the eagles be gathered together. ²⁹Immediately after the tribulation of those days shall the sun be darkened, and the moon shall not give her light, and the stars shall fall from heaven, and the powers of the heavens shall be shaken: ³⁰And then shall appear the sign of the Son of man in heaven: and then shall all the tribes of the earth mourn, and they shall see the Son of man coming in the clouds of heaven with power and great glory. ³¹And he shall send his angels with a great sound of a trumpet, and they shall gather together his elect from the four winds, from one end of heaven to the other. "

In this section Jesus was referring to the end time and His warning was directed especially towards the identification of false christs appearing here and there. Recently it is becoming evident that this phenomenon is on the increase as popular books and films are launched misinterpreting the true mission and character of Jesus Christ. We are forewarned that Satan himself will appear as an angel of light, speaking the same words as Jesus, performing "signs and wonders".

Jesus gave a clear indication that His second coming would not be a secret one, or secret rapture as some might put it, but very visual (as lightning) and audible (trumpet and angels with a great sound). It would be witnessed by the whole world. His angels shall gather together his elect. Those who died in Him will be resurrected from the grave and those who would still be alive would be changed.[275] There would be a time of great tribulation just before the end time, as never before in history. [276]

> "[32] Now learn a parable of the fig tree; When his branch is yet tender, and putteth forth leaves, ye know that summer is nigh: [33] So likewise ye, when ye shall see all these things, know that it is near, even at the doors. [34] Verily I say unto you, This generation shall not pass, till all these things be fulfilled."

The followers of Jesus were to keep watch for these events and study the signs of the time. Many who lived in the time of Jesus Christ would still be alive when the destruction of Jerusalem would take place nearly forty years later. According to historical tradition all the Christians left Jerusalem before its destruction which was preceded by a siege.[277]

> "[35] Heaven and earth shall pass away, but my words shall not pass away. [36] But of that day and hour knoweth no man, no, not the angels of heaven, but my Father only. [37] But as the days of Noe were, so shall also the coming of the Son of man be. [38] For as in the days that

---

[275] 1 Thes.4:13-17
[276] Rev.15 & 16
[277] Eze.13:16

were before the flood they were eating and drinking, marrying and giving in marriage, until the day that Noe entered into the ark, [39]And knew not until the flood came, and took them all away; so shall also the coming of the Son of man be."

The exact date of Jesus' second coming would not be known by man. In this section Jesus referred again to the end of time when people would carry on with their business as usual as in the days of Noah, when they also did not take his warnings to heart and were drowned in the flood. Jesus also gave credibility to the account of Noah and the redemption of those who were saved by God in the ark.

"[40]Then shall two be in the field; the one shall be taken, and the other left. [41]Two women shall be grinding at the mill; the one shall be taken, and the other left."

Verses 40 and 41 refer to the people living at the time of Jesus' second coming. His children will join Him in the clouds while the other inhabitants will be destroyed.[278] But firstly His children who died in Him will rise from their graves.[279]

"[42]Watch therefore: for ye know not what hour your Lord doth come. [43]But know this, that if the goodman of the house had known in what watch the thief would come, he would have watched, and would not have suffered his house to be broken up. [44]Therefore be ye also ready: for in such an hour as ye think not the Son of man cometh. [45]Who then is a faithful and wise servant, whom his lord hath made

---

[278] Matt.25:41
[279] 1 Thes.4:16, 1 Cor.15:20

ruler over his household, to give them meat in due season? ⁴⁶Blessed is that servant, whom his lord when he cometh shall find so doing. ⁴⁷Verily I say unto you, That he shall make him ruler over all his goods. ⁴⁸But and if that evil servant shall say in his heart, My lord delayeth his coming; ⁴⁹And shall begin to smite his fellowservants, and to eat and drink with the drunken; ⁵⁰The lord of that servant shall come in a day when he looketh not for him, and in an hour that he is not aware of, ⁵¹And shall cut him asunder, and appoint him his portion with the hypocrites: there shall be weeping and gnashing of teeth."

In the preceding section Jesus illustrated through a short parable how some will be faithful and watchful until the end, while others will influence people to stop being watchful and will be caught unawares when Jesus comes.[280] The second coming of Christ will surprise many.[281] The idea was often repeated by Jesus – He will come when many will not be ready. It is interesting to note that the servant knew that the master would come, but got listless due to what he saw as a delay. This gives the impression that Jesus was not referring to people who did not know about Him, but to Christians who knew that He was going to return. The idea that many will be so caught up with the things of the world, e.g. eating and drinking, at the coming of Jesus, was also described in Luke 21:34:

> *"³⁴And take heed to yourselves, lest at any time your hearts be overcharged with surfeiting, and drunkenness, and cares of this life, and so that day come upon you unawares. ³⁵For as a snare shall it*

---
[280] Rev.3:3
[281] 1 Thes.5:3

come on all them that dwell on the face of the whole earth. ³⁶Watch ye therefore, and pray always, that ye may be accounted worthy to escape all these things that shall come to pass, and to stand before the Son of man."

Matthew 25

Jesus concluded His formal teaching by the telling of His last two parables and end-time prediction as recorded in Matthew 25. Firstly, He told the very well-known parable of the ten virgins (vs.1 – 13) and secondly the parable of the talents (vs.14 – 30). Finally Jesus described the closing scenes of earth's history – two groups left on account of their own choices and deeds and the compensation that each group will receive.

"¹Then shall the kingdom of heaven be likened unto ten virgins, which took their lamps, and went forth to meet the bridegroom. ²And five of them were wise, and five were foolish. ³They that were foolish took their lamps, and took no oil with them: ⁴But the wise took oil in their vessels with their lamps. ⁵While the bridegroom tarried, they all slumbered and slept. ⁶And at midnight there was a cry made, Behold, the bridegroom cometh; go ye out to meet him. ⁷Then all those virgins arose, and trimmed their lamps. ⁸And the foolish said unto the wise, Give us of your oil; for our lamps are gone out. ⁹But the wise answered, saying, Not so; lest there be not enough for us and you: but go ye rather to them that sell, and buy for yourselves. ¹⁰And while they went to buy, the bridegroom came; and they that were ready went in with him to the marriage: and the door was shut. ¹¹Afterward came also the other virgins, saying, Lord, Lord, open to us. ¹²But he answered and said, Verily I say unto you, I know you not. ¹³Watch therefore, for ye know neither the day nor the hour wherein the Son of man cometh."

According to the interpretation of the symbols already used by Jesus and other Scriptural references the following conclusions can be made as to the meaning of the different entities in the parable (see table 9).

So, although the foolish maidens made a promising start, they could not endure to the end. They made a habit of relying on others. But in the end every person will be responsible for him- or herself and nobody would be able to just tag along. Do not think that if you have a godly wife or husband, for example, you have automatic entrance to heaven. Only the truly committed will be ready for His second coming. They will have the Holy Spirit in their hearts and their characters will shine forth as children of God.

The reaction of Jesus *"I know you not"* is very significant. To know someone is to have a personal relationship with that person. To know Jesus Christ as your personal Savior would reflect in your behavior. Out of gratitude for the high price that He paid for your salvation, you would be doing His will – be obedient and do the things He commanded. The law that Jesus promoted is the same law as in the Old Testament, for it reflects the character of God. Jesus Christ is part of the Godhead and nothing He proclaimed differed from that which was already written in the Old Testament.

TABLE 9 THE MEANING OF THE DIFFERENT ENTITIES IN THE PARABLE OF THE TEN VIRGINS

Symbol	Meaning
Ten	Easy number to remember
Virgins	Those who profess a pure and true faith in Jesus[282]
Five wise and five foolish	The wise virgins were filled with the Holy Spirit and led by Him in their preparation of the Lord's second coming, while the foolish virgins did not take the warnings seriously.
Lamps	The Word of God [283]
Bridegroom	Jesus Christ[284]
Oil	The Holy Spirit [285]
Extra oil in vessel	They were truly committed, giving their lives to Jesus Christ
He tarried – they slept	He took longer than they expected – they became inactive/weary/not attentive
Midnight cry (Rev.14:6-8)	A wake-up call that He was coming
Give us of your oil	Every person will be responsible for him/her own choices and cannot assume that he/she can go through to the wedding on the merits of

---

[282] Gal.2:20
[283] Ps.119:105
[284] Matt.9:15
[285] Acts 10:38 (anointed with the Holy Spirit)

	others
They went to buy, the bridegroom came and the door was shut	There comes a cut-off time when con-version will no more take place.[286] e should use our time wisely, serving the Lord.
They cried that He should open the door, but He replied that He did not know them	The phrase "I know you not", was a repetition of what Jesus told them in Matthew 7:21-23
Watch therefore …	Be alert: nobody knows the time of His Second Coming[287]

According to Jesus' prayer for his disciples to inherit eternal life means we should **know God** (John 17:3):

> "*3 And this is life eternal, that they might know thee the only true God, and Jesus Christ, whom thou hast sent.*"

And in John 17:25, 26 Jesus proclaims that He knows the Father:

> "*25 O righteous Father, the world hath not known thee: but I have known thee, and these have known that thou hast sent me. 26 And I have declared unto them thy name, and will declare [it]: that the love wherewith thou hast loved me may be in them, and I in them.*"

To get to know God we have to study his Word **and obey it**. 1 Joh.2:3 states:

---

[286] Rev.14:15; Rev.22:11
[287] Matt.24:44

"And hereby we do know that we know him, if we keep his commandments."

The next parable deals with the work of spreading the Gospel – obeying the command given in Matt.28:19.

"¹⁴For the kingdom of heaven is as a man travelling into a far country, who called his own servants, and delivered unto them his goods. ¹⁵And unto one he gave five talents, to another two, and to another one; to every man according to his several ability; and straightway took his journey. ¹⁶Then he that had received the five talents went and traded with the same, and made them other five talents. ¹⁷And likewise he that had received two, he also gained other two. ¹⁸But he that had received one went and digged in the earth, and hid his lord's money. ¹⁹After a long time the lord of those servants cometh, and reckoneth with them. ²⁰And so he that had received five talents came and brought other five talents, saying, Lord, thou deliveredst unto me five talents: behold, I have gained beside them five talents more. ²¹ His lord said unto him, Well done, thou good and faithful servant: thou hast been faithful over a few things, I will make thee ruler over many things: enter thou into the joy of thy lord. ²² He also that had received two talents came and said, Lord, thou deliveredst unto me two talents: behold, I have gained two other talents beside them. ²³His lord said unto him, Well done, good and faithful servant; thou hast been faithful over a few things, I will make thee ruler over many things: enter thou into the joy of thy lord. ²⁴Then he which had received the one talent came and said, Lord, I knew thee that thou art an hard man, reaping where thou hast not sown, and gathering where thou hast not strawed: ²⁵And I was afraid, and went and hid thy talent in the earth: lo, there thou hast that is thine. ²⁶ His lord answered and said unto him, Thou wicked and slothful servant, thou knewest that I reap where I sowed not, and gather where I have not strawed: ²⁷Thou oughtest therefore to have put my money to the exchangers, and then at my coming I should have received mine own with usury. ²⁸Take therefore the talent from

him, and give it unto him which hath ten talents. ²⁹For unto every one that hath shall be given, and he shall have abundance: but from him that hath not shall be taken away even that which he hath. ³⁰And cast ye the unprofitable servant into outer darkness: there shall be weeping and gnashing of teeth. "

In this parable Jesus stressed that He would be expecting his servants to be busy spreading the Gospel and serving Him until He comes again. The Master wanted his shares to increase and this was also a test for his servants. The talents would be the special gifts of the Spirit that Jesus' followers would receive to use in His service. (Eph.4:11-13).

The first servant proved to be very diligent and he received the master's approval. Jesus is glad when He sees our commitment. To the servant who received two talents He gave the same words of appraisal: "Well done". God does not expect more of us than what we are capable of. [288]

The unfaithful servant tried to put the blame on the Master. He was unwilling to accept responsibility and to commit himself to the service of the Lord.

Everyone will receive the punishment according to his own choices and works, which will be the natural outflow of the choices made. The one talent of the unfaithful servant was taken away and given to the one who received ten talents. Although nobody is saved through works, they will be recognized by

---

[288] 2 Cor.8:12; Luke 19:24

their works: if their conversion was real or fake. This was clearly illustrated by Jesus in his last parable.

> "^{31}When the Son of man shall come in his glory, and all the holy angels with him, then shall he sit upon the throne of his glory: ^{32}And before him shall be gathered all nations: and he shall separate them one from another, as a shepherd divideth his sheep from the goats: ^{33}And he shall set the sheep on his right hand, but the goats on the left. ^{34}Then shall the King say unto them on his right hand, Come, ye blessed of my Father, inherit the kingdom prepared for you from the foundation of the world: ^{35}For I was an hungred, and ye gave me meat: I was thirsty, and ye gave me drink: I was a stranger, and ye took me in: ^{36}Naked, and ye clothed me: I was sick, and ye visited me: I was in prison, and ye came unto me. ^{37}Then shall the righteous answer him, saying, Lord, when saw we thee an hungred, and fed thee? or thirsty, and gave thee drink? ^{38} When saw we thee a stranger, and took thee in? or naked, and clothed thee? ^{39} Or when saw we thee sick, or in prison, and came unto thee? ^{40}And the King shall answer and say unto them, Verily I say unto you, Inasmuch as ye have done it unto one of the least of these my brethren, ye have done it unto me. ^{41}Then shall he say also unto them on the left hand, Depart from me, ye cursed, into everlasting fire, prepared for the devil and his angels: ^{42}For I was an hungred, and ye gave me no meat: I was thirsty, and ye gave me no drink: ^{43}I was a stranger, and ye took me not in: naked, and ye clothed me not: sick, and in prison, and ye visited me not. ^{44}Then shall they also answer him, saying, Lord, when saw we thee an hungred, or athirst, or a stranger, or naked, or sick, or in prison, and did not minister unto thee? ^{45}Then shall he answer them, saying, Verily I say unto you, Inasmuch as ye did it not to one of the least of these, ye did it not to me. ^{46}And these shall go away into everlasting punishment: but the righteous into life eternal."

Jesus put it in clear and easy language on what the final judgment will be based. In using the words: Son of Man,[289] Christ was using one of His favorite

expressions in referring to Himself. It appears eighty times in the Gospels. The title designates Him as the incarnate Christ.[290] It indicates the unification between Creator and creation. The sons of men can now also become sons of God through faith in Jesus Christ.[291]

When Jesus comes again in all His glory He will come to inaugurate his eternal kingdom forever.[292] The angels will be present.[293] He shall sit as King, Priest and Judge on a throne.[294] An investigative judgment would have taken place before His coming, resulting in a final separation between the sheep and the goats at His appearance.[295] In other words, the acts of kindness or unkindness would be weighed in the light of a person's confession of faith in Christ as his personal Savior.

The scene Jesus was depicting was that of the final judgment.[296] On his right hand stand those who will receive honor and blessing, but on his left hand are those who will be punished. The ones on his right hand will enter into possession of property – the new earth, that which was God's original plan for

---

[289] Mark 2:10
[290] Joh.1:14; Phil.2:6-8
[291] Joh.1:12; Gal.4:3-7; 1 Joh.3:1,2
[292] Dan.7:14; Rev.11:15; Mat.4:17
[293] Dan.7:10; Rev.5:11
[294] Zech.6:12,13
[295] Rev.22:12
[296] Rev.20:11-15

this world at the beginning of creation. He will rule supreme.[297]

In verses 35-40 Jesus explained that those on his right had practiced the deeds which were the natural outflow of their true conversion – the principle of love in action. He identified with the down-trodden when He was on earth, and so his followers would do if their love for Him was true.[298] This principle was also illustrated by the parable of the Good Samaritan.[299]The people on His right did not even realize that they did these good deeds, as it came so naturally to them to act kindly when the opportunity arose.

The people on the left hand side of Jesus would be equally surprised as to the outcome of the judgment and never even realized how unkind their behavior was towards others. Every time they looked the other way when they saw someone in need, they acted in abject selfishness and Jesus experienced it as if it was done to Himself.

The everlasting fire in verse 41 refers to an unquenchable fire. It does not indicate that the fire is going to be permanent, but that its results will be permanent.[300] The same kind of scenario described the destruction of Sodom and Gomorrah where there was also mention of an eternal fire[301] – but it

---

[297] Dan.7:27; Matt.6:10; Luke 12:32, Rev.21:3
[298] Gal.6:2; 1 Joh.3:14-19
[299] Luke 10:30-37
[300] Jude 1:7; Matt.3:12; Matt.5:22; 2 Pet.3:10-12; Rev.20:10; Eze.22:31

is obviously not still burning today. It is one of the greatest fables the devil devised - the so-called hell and that this is a place where he will burn sinners forever. As mentioned in Matthew 10:28, it is God who judges and ultimately destroys those who reject his love, including the devil and his angels.[302]

The lot of the devil is also described in other sections of the Bible.[303]

The ultimate reward for the righteous will be to inherit the earth made new and be in the presence of God for ever.[304] His children are eagerly waiting for that day.[305]

> **Matthew 26**
> *"¹And it came to pass, when Jesus had finished all these sayings, he said unto his disciples, ²Ye know that after two days is the feast of the passover, and the Son of man is betrayed to be crucified ⁶Now when Jesus was in Bethany, in the house of Simon the leper, ⁷There came unto him a woman having an alabaster box of very precious ointment, and poured it on his head, as he sat at meat. ⁸But when his disciples saw it, they had indignation, saying, To what purpose is this waste? ⁹For this ointment might have been sold for much, and given to the poor. ¹⁰When Jesus understood it, he said unto them, Why trouble ye the woman? for she hath wrought a good work upon me. ¹¹For ye have the poor always with you; but me ye have not always. ¹²For in that she hath poured this ointment on my body, she did it for my burial. ¹³Verily I say unto you, Wheresoever this gospel*

---

[301] Jude 1:7, 2 Pet.2:6
[302] Rev.20:7-10; 2 Pet.2:4
[303] 2 Pet.2:4, Jude 1:6,7
[304] John 3:16; Rom.6:23; Rev.21:7
[305] Rev.22:20

shall be preached in the whole world, there shall also this, that this woman hath done, be told for a memorial of her. "

The woman was Mary, the sister of Lazarus and Martha, and the ointment was spikenard, a costly and aromatic oil, according to John 12:1-3. According to Matthew and Mark, she poured it on Jesus' head, while in Luke and John it was mentioned that she poured it onto his feet. There is no reason, however, that she could not have done both.

In Jesus' reply to the disciples' complaint about the cost of the ointment, He acknowledged her deed as of great importance concerning his coming death and burial.

> "[17]Now the first day of the feast of unleavened bread the disciples came to Jesus, saying unto him, Where wilt thou that we prepare for thee to eat the passover? [18]And he said, Go into the city to such a man, and say unto him, The Master saith, My time is at hand; I will keep the passover at thy house with my disciples. [19]And the disciples did as Jesus had appointed them; and they made ready the passover. [20]Now when the even was come, he sat down with the twelve. [21]And as they did eat, he said, Verily I say unto you, that one of you shall betray me. [22]And they were exceeding sorrowful, and began every one of them to say unto him, Lord, is it I? [23]And he answered and said, He that dippeth his hand with me in the dish, the same shall betray me. [24] The Son of man goeth as it is written of him: but woe unto that man by whom the Son of man is betrayed! it had been good for that man if he had not been born. [25]Then Judas, which betrayed him, answered and said, Master, is it I? He said unto him, Thou hast said."

Jesus foretold that Judas would betray him, even before Judas went out to do the final betrayal. Herewith Jesus gave Judas a final chance to repent. When Judas realized that Jesus knew of his betrayal he left the room and went to meet with the Jewish leaders.

> *"26And as they were eating, Jesus took bread, and blessed it, and brake it, and gave it to the disciples, and said, Take, eat; this is my body. 27And he took the cup, and gave thanks, and gave it to them, saying, Drink ye all of it; 28For this is my blood of the new testament, which is shed for many for the remission of sins. 29But I say unto you, I will not drink henceforth of this fruit of the vine, until that day when I drink it new with you in my Father's kingdom. 30And when they had sung an hymn, they went out into the mount of Olives. 31Then saith Jesus unto them, all ye shall be offended because of me this night: for it is written, I will smite the shepherd, and the sheep of the flock shall be scattered abroad. 32But after I am risen again, I will go before you into Galilee. 33Peter answered and said unto him, Though all men shall be offended because of thee, yet will I never be offended. 34Jesus said unto him, Verily I say unto thee, That this night, before the cock crow, thou shalt deny me thrice. 35Peter said unto him, Though I should die with thee, yet will I not deny thee. Likewise also said all the disciples."*

In Matthew 26 Jesus made important predictions and statements concerning everything that had to do with his impending death on the cross and the Passover. He also instituted Holy Communion.

What followed from verse 36 was exactly as Jesus predicted. The group went to Gethsemane and Jesus was suffering greatly, because He could feel the burden of the sins of the world resting on Him. In asking the disciples to support Him with their prayers, we are shown the importance of intercessory prayer.

> "Then cometh Jesus with them unto a place called Gethsemane, and saith unto the disciples, Sit ye here, while I go and pray yonder. ³⁷And he took with him Peter and the two sons of Zebedee, and began to be sorrowful and very heavy. ³⁸Then saith he unto them, My soul is exceeding sorrowful, even unto death: tarry ye here, and watch with me. ³⁹And he went a little further, and fell on his face, and prayed, saying, O my Father, if it be possible, let this cup pass from me: nevertheless not as I will, but as thou wilt. ⁴⁰And he cometh unto the disciples, and findeth them asleep, and saith unto Peter, What, could ye not watch with me one hour? ⁴¹Watch and pray, that ye enter not into temptation: the spirit indeed is willing, but the flesh is weak. ⁴²He went away again the second time, and prayed, saying, O my Father, if this cup may not pass away from me, except I drink it, thy will be done."

The burden of carrying the sins of the world and his forth coming trail was putting Jesus under tremendous stress:

> "My soul is exceeding sorrowful, even unto death "(verse 38).

In other words He felt as if He was dying and that his human body would not be able to take it. He prayed to God to take it away – but at the same time submitted to the will of God, His Father.

> "⁴³And he came and found them asleep again: for their eyes were heavy. ⁴⁴And he left them, and went away again, and prayed the third time, saying the same words. ⁴⁵Then cometh he to his disciples, and saith unto them, Sleep on now, and take your rest: behold, the hour is at hand, and the Son of man is betrayed into the hands of

sinners. ⁴⁶Rise, let us be going: behold, he is at hand that doth betray me."

Predictions made by Jesus in Matthew 26:

- After two days it would be the Passover and He would be crucified (verse 2).
- The anointing by the woman was for his burial (verse 12).
- One of his disciples, namely Judas, was going to betray Him (verse 24, 25).
- After he instituted Holy Communion He said that He would not drink the fruit of the vine until He would drink it in his Father's kingdom (verses 26-29).
- He quoted from Zech.13:7 in saying that all of them would stumble that night (verse 31).
- He said that He would be raised after his death and would meet the disciples in Galilee (verse 32).
- He predicted that Peter would betray Him three times before the cock crows (verse 34).

What followed from verse 47 was also exactly as Jesus predicted from being betrayed by Judas up to the point where they all fled and left Jesus with the mob that came to arrest Him. He still gave an important lesson to Peter (John 18:10) after he (Peter) cut off the ear of one of the people in the mob and Jesus healed the ear again: Jesus said:

"Put up again thy sword into his place: for all they that take the sword shall perish with the sword" (Matt.26:52).

Herewith Jesus also explained that those enlisting for His army must understand that it is a battle of the mind and not to be enforced by physical fighting and bloodshed.

> "*47And while he yet spake, lo, Judas, one of the twelve, came, and with him a great multitude with swords and staves, from the chief priests and elders of the people. 48Now he that betrayed him gave them a sign, saying, Whomsoever I shall kiss, that same is he: hold him fast. 49And forthwith he came to Jesus, and said, Hail, master; and kissed him. 50And Jesus said unto him, Friend, wherefore art thou come? Then came they, and laid hands on Jesus, and took him. 51And, behold, one of them which were with Jesus stretched out his hand, and drew his sword, and struck a servant of the high priest's, and smote off his ear. 52Then said Jesus unto him, Put up again thy sword into his place: for all they that take the sword shall perish with the sword. 53 Thinkest thou that I cannot now pray to my Father, and he shall presently give me more than twelve legions of angels? 54But how then shall the scriptures be fulfilled, that thus it must be?"*

Jesus explained to Peter that the battle is not a physical one, for in that case God could have sent legions of angels to protect Him. According to Luke 22:51, Jesus healed the servant's ear.

> "*55In that same hour said Jesus to the multitudes, Are ye come out as against a thief with swords and staves for to take me? I sat daily with you teaching in the temple, and ye laid no hold on me. 56But all this was done, that the scriptures of the prophets might be fulfilled. Then all the disciples forsook him, and fled."*

After Jesus was betrayed by Judas, He was taken to appear before Caiaphas and from then on did not say much. He was confronted by Caiaphas in verse 63:

> "⁶³ And the high priest answered and said unto him, I adjure thee by the living God, that thou tell us whether thou be the Christ, the Son of God."

Jesus answered in verse 64:

> "⁶⁴ Hereafter shall ye see the Son of man sitting on the right hand of power, and coming in the clouds of heaven."

This would have been blasphemy if it wasn't the truth. But Caiaphas would not accept the truth and therefore condemned Jesus for speaking blasphemy. He tore his clothes and the bystanders agreed with him: Jesus is guilty and they spat in his face and hit Him with sticks.

Then Peter, from the court yard where he was viewing the proceedings, betrayed Jesus by denying three times that he was one of Jesus' disciples. Directly after he denied Jesus for the third time, the cock crowed, and Peter remembered Jesus' words:

> "³⁴Jesus said unto him, Verily I say unto thee, That this night, before the cock crow, thou shalt deny me thrice."

He went outside and cried bitterly.

Matthew 26 and 27 in prophecy

In Matthew 26 and 27 an account is given of the trial of Jesus, His crucifixion and burial. Everything happened as was predicted by Him and several prophets of old. As the events took place the scriptural reference of the prediction will be placed in brackets.

- Matt.26: 60: False witnesses were brought before court (Ps.27:12).
- Matt. 26:63: When he was accused, Jesus kept quiet (Isa. 53:7).
- Matt.26:64: Jesus answered:

    "Hereafter shall ye see the Son of man sitting on the right hand of power, and coming in the clouds of heaven" (Dan.7:13, 14).

- Matt.26:67: They spat in his face and hit him (Isa.50:6).
- Matt.26:75: Peter denied the Lord three times, as Jesus predicted he would (Matt.26:34).
- Matt.27:9: Judas betrayed Jesus for thirty pieces of silver, but when he realized what he had done, he threw it back at the Jewish leaders and they bought the potter's field as was predicted by Zechariah (Zech.11:12,13).
- Matt.27:26: Jesus was beaten and given over to be crucified by Pontius Pilate (Isa.53:5).
- Matt. 27:27: The soldiers put a scarlet robe on Jesus, a crown of thorns on His head and a reed in His hand, mocking Him saying: "Hail King of the Jews!" (Isa.53:3).
- Matt.27:34: They gave Him vinegar and gall to drink (Ps.69:21).
- Jesus predicted His crucifixion in Matt.26:2.

- Matt.27:35: They crucified Him and also two robbers on each side (Isa.53:12).
- Matt.27:35: They casted lots over His garment (Ps.22:18).
- Matt.27:39: Passersby were wagging their heads and mockingly declared that if He was the son of God, He should come down from the cross. (Ps.22:7, 8, Isa.37:22,23).
- Matt.27:46: His very last words:

  "Eli, Eli, lama sabachthani? that is to say, My God, my God, why hast thou forsaken me? was prophesied by David" (Ps.22:1).

- They buried Jesus in a tomb that was donated by a rich man (Isa.53:9).
- After Jesus' resurrection he told Mary Magdalene and the other Mary to go and tell his disciples that He has risen and will meet them in Galilee. This He also foretold in Matthew 26:32.
- The last words of Jesus reported according to the gospel of Matthew were His final directive to the disciples:

  "[18] And Jesus came and spake unto them, saying, All power is given unto me in heaven and in earth. [19] Go ye therefore, and teach all nations, baptizing them in the name of the Father, and of the Son, and of the Holy Ghost: [20] Teaching them to observe all things whatsoever I have commanded you: and, lo, I am with you alway, [even] unto the end of the world. Amen."

Jesus gave them the assurance that He had achieved what He came to do:

"All power is given unto me in heaven and in earth" **and a promise never to leave them alone,"** *I am with you alway, [even] unto the end of the world".*

This will be fulfilled by the indwelling and guidance of the Holy Spirit. Jesus here also emphasized the Trinity of Father, Son and Holy Ghost.

Jesus included three verbs in this section: go, teach, baptize. He ended his teaching by telling them *"to observe all things whatsoever I have commanded you".*

Chapter 7
Important short quotes and statements spoken by Jesus

In this chapter some of Jesus' short quotes and edifying phrases not yet commented upon, will be discussed. These are also very note-worthy as they contain important insights.

> **Matthew 3**
> "*¹³Then cometh Jesus from Galilee to Jordan unto John, to be baptized of him. ¹⁴But John forbad him, saying, I have need to be baptized of thee, and comest thou to me? ¹⁵And Jesus answering said unto him, Suffer it to be so now: for thus it becometh us to fulfil all righteousness.*"

Whereas baptism to us is a public declaration of our confession and washing away of sins, it would not be fitting for Jesus to undergo this action as He was sinless. In this regard John the Baptist was correct in stating that he should rather have been baptized by Christ.

However Jesus had to go through with the action as an example for us, showing us the right way. Thereafter He received the anointing of the Holy Spirit and the blessing of the Father to support Him in his ministry that was about to start.

> "*¹⁶ And Jesus, when he was baptized, went up straightway out of the water: and, lo, the heavens were opened unto him, and he saw the*

Spirit of God descending like a dove, and lighting upon him: [17] *And lo a voice from heaven, saying, This is my beloved Son, in whom I am well pleased."*

Baptism of babies is not Biblical and not in line with its teaching. In Acts 2:38 Peter urges his listeners:

"Repent, and be baptized every one of you in the name of Jesus Christ for the remission of sins, and ye shall receive the gift of the Holy Ghost."

It is not possible for a baby to repent. Some Christians believe that the baptism of babies came in the place of circumcision. Why then would they baptize little girls?

It remains a mystery: why do people always do things their own way when Jesus directly or through the teachings in the Bible gave direct, straightforward instructions? It started with Cain who did not follow God's instruction regarding which sacrifice to bring. (Hebr.11:4). The sacrifice of a lamb was to point forward to Jesus who would be sacrificed for our sins. But Cain thought he would be cleverer and sacrificed fruit (Gen.4:3). 1 John 3:12 states that:

"Not as Cain, [who] was of that wicked one, and slew his brother. And wherefore slew he him? Because his own works were evil, and his brother's righteous."

Yes, there we have the answer. Under the influence of the devil and thinking that he knew better than God (self-righteous) Cain sinned.

So why can't we just follow the instructions in the Bible regarding baptism. Jesus set the example and was baptized. He was immersed in the river. The symbolic act for us who thereby declare our washing away of sin – the dying of the old person and coming up as a newborn person in Christ.

Babies can be brought to the church and prayed for. This is a good practice, especially for the parents to commit themselves to bring up the child in the ways of the Lord.

But every person has to make a decision to repent and be baptized when he/she is old enough to understand the full implications thereof. They have to believe that Jesus Christ died on the cross for them personally.

Matthew 4
"⁴But he answered and said, It is written, Man shall not live by bread alone, but by every word that proceedeth out of the mouth of God. ⁵Then the devil taketh him up into the holy city, and setteth him on a pinnacle of the temple, ⁶And saith unto him, If thou be the Son of God, cast thyself down: for it is written, He shall give his angels charge concerning thee: and in their hands they shall bear thee up, lest at any time thou dash thy foot against a stone. ⁷Jesus said unto him, It is written again, Thou shalt not tempt the Lord thy God. ⁸Again, the devil taketh him up into an exceeding high mountain, and

sheweth him all the kingdoms of the world, and the glory of them; ⁹And saith unto him, All these things will I give thee, if thou wilt fall down and worship me. ¹⁰Then saith Jesus unto him, Get thee hence, Satan: for it is written, Thou shalt worship the Lord thy God, and him only shalt thou serve. ¹¹Then the devil leaveth him, and, behold, angels came and ministered unto him."

Being tempted by the devil, Jesus quoted from Scripture demonstrating his thorough knowledge of the books of the Old Testament. See page 3 at the introduction of this book of the books He quoted from, according to the Gospel of Matthew.

In verse 4[306] Jesus accentuates the importance of spiritual matters above the physical. In verse 7[307] He quotes from Deut.6:16 stating that you should not tempt God – in a way it comes down to playing games with God, expecting Him to demonstrate his power just to prove it.

In verse 10[308] Jesus referred the devil to the first commandment. Then the devil left Him. Interestingly enough, the devil also quoted from Scripture in verse 16, trying to trick Jesus. We should take note of the fact that the devil also knows the Bible and would always try to get people to misunderstand or misinterpret it.

Matthew 4
"¹⁸And Jesus, walking by the sea of Galilee, saw two brethren, Simon called Peter, and Andrew his brother, casting a net into the

---

[306] Deut.8:3
[307] Deut.6:16
[308] Deut.6:13; Ex.20:2,3

sea: for they were fishers. ⁱ⁹And he saith unto them, Follow me, and I will make you fishers of men."

A new dispensation was started known to us today as an evangelistic outreach ministry. This was a totally foreign idea to the people of Israel up to that time. They would cling to their inclusive ideas of being chosen by God to the exclusion of others.

From that time onwards the good news of salvation through faith in Jesus Christ, the crucified and risen Messiah, would be proclaimed first to the Jews and then to the whole world. Everyone who believes in Him as their personal Savior can have eternal life.

Matthew 8
"¹⁰When Jesus heard it, he marvelled, and said to them that followed, Verily I say unto you, I have not found so great faith, no, not in Israel. ¹¹And I say unto you, That many shall come from the east and west, and shall sit down with Abraham, and Isaac, and Jacob, in the kingdom of heaven. ¹²But the children of the kingdom shall be cast out into outer darkness: there shall be weeping and gnashing of teeth. ¹³And Jesus said unto the centurion, Go thy way; and as thou hast believed, so be it done unto thee. And his servant was healed in the selfsame hour."

Here Jesus commented on the faith of outsiders, in this case a Roman centurion. They who had the Holy Scriptures and the prophecies would not accept or recognize Him as the Messiah.

"¹⁰...I have not found so great faith, no, not in Israel."

He then prophesied that

"¹²...the children of the kingdom shall be cast out into outer darkness:"

Thus He pronounced a judgment on the *"children of the kingdom"* for their lack of faith.

Matthew 9

"²And, behold, they brought to him a man sick of the palsy, lying on a bed: and Jesus seeing their faith said unto the sick of the palsy; Son, be of good cheer; thy sins be forgiven thee. ³And, behold, certain of the scribes said within themselves, This man blasphemeth. ⁴And Jesus knowing their thoughts said, Wherefore think ye evil in your hearts? ⁵For whether is easier, to say, Thy sins be forgiven thee; or to say, Arise, and walk? ⁶But that ye may know that the Son of man hath power on earth to forgive sins, (then saith he to the sick of the palsy,) Arise, take up thy bed, and go unto thine house."

In this section Jesus deliberately said to the man with palsy —*"thy sins be forgiven..."* thereby demonstrating that He was indeed God. Of course the scribes would be affronted, as they could not recognize the Messiah in front of them, due to their hardness of heart.

Jesus showed them that He did things this way around for a purpose: it could have been much easier and less controversial just to have said to the man: take your bed and go. But He wanted them to understand his divinity. No human being has the power or the authority to forgive sins.

"¹¹And when the Pharisees saw it, they said unto his disciples, Why eateth your Master with publicans and sinners? ¹²But when Jesus heard that, he said unto them, They that be whole need not a physician, but they that are sick. ¹³But go ye and learn what that

meaneth, I will have mercy, and not sacrifice: for I am not come to call the righteous, but sinners to repentance.

In their comment: *"Why eateth your Master with publicans and sinners?"* the Pharisees demonstrated their condescending attitude. Jesus set them straight with the beautiful answer: *"I am not come to call the righteous, but sinners to repentance".*

More than once did Jesus repeat the saying: *"I will have mercy, and not sacrifice".*[309] As a merciful God, He expects his followers to be merciful. This was also demonstrated by way of parables[310] and in the Lord's Prayer.[311]

> *"14Then came to him the disciples of John, saying, Why do we and the Pharisees fast oft, but thy disciples fast not? 15And Jesus said unto them, Can the children of the bridechamber mourn, as long as the bridegroom is with them? but the days will come, when the bridegroom shall be taken from them, and then shall they fast. 16 No man putteth a piece of new cloth unto an old garment, for that which is put in to fill it up taketh from the garment, and the rent is made worse. 17Neither do men put new wine into old bottles: else the bottles break, and the wine runneth out, and the bottles perish: but they put new wine into new bottles, and both are preserved."*

The scribes had very strict ways whereby they fasted twice a week. They thought that these pious ways would appease God. We know that John the Baptist also had a very simplistic way of living and can assume that his disciples followed him in this

---
[309] Hosea 6:6
[310] Matt.19:21
[311] Matt.6:12

matter. Jesus explained that He came to show them a new approach (new wine) and that the old ways were not what God wanted (mercy more than sacrifice).

Jesus gave a clear explanation to the Pharisees' question on why his disciples did not fast. While He (the bridegroom) was still with them it was not a time for fasting. After his death, there would be more time for earnest fasting and prayer.

> *"²⁷And when Jesus departed thence, two blind men followed him, crying, and saying, Thou Son of David, have mercy on us. ²⁸And when he was come into the house, the blind men came to him: and Jesus saith unto them, Believe ye that I am able to do this? They said unto him, Yea, Lord. ²⁹Then touched he their eyes, saying, According to your faith be it unto you. ³⁰And their eyes were opened; and Jesus straitly charged them, saying, See that no man know it."*

The words of Jesus: *"Believe ye that I am able to do this?"* are very illuminating for us on how faith works. Such simple words, but with such significant meaning: if He is able to do this miracle it would imply that He is the Messiah like they were indeed witnessing: *"Thou Son of David"*. They believed with childlike faith and were healed.

> *"³⁶But when he saw the multitudes, he was moved with compassion on them, because they fainted, and were scattered abroad, as sheep having no shepherd. ³⁷Then saith he unto his disciples, The harvest truly is plenteous, but the labourers are few; ³⁸Pray ye therefore the Lord of the harvest, that he will send forth labourers into his harvest."*

In the first place it is important to note that Jesus was moved with compassion – He really identified with the needs of the people.

We are encouraged to pray for laborers to do the Lord's work. There are many who are ready to accept the Lord's gift of salvation, but humans are needed to assist them in making their final choice. God's Holy Spirit will prepare the crops and we can rejoice in participating in the harvest feast.

The very last word spoken by Jesus before dying on the cross, according to John 19:30 were: *"It is finished".*

> *"When Jesus therefore had received the vinegar, he said, It is finished: and he bowed his head, and gave up the ghost."*

We know that John who was standing close to the cross supporting Jesus' mother, would have been able to hear these words, not recorded by the other gospel writers.

With these words Jesus died. No visual illustration can ever truthfully portray the extent of his suffering before and on the cross. The anguish of his heart will never be fully understood by men. He was separated from his friends – even betrayed by them. He was unrightfully accused by the people of political and church powers. He bore the weight of the sins of the world on his shoulders and eventually was separated from his beloved Father – his one unswerving dependable source of power. He cried out, (Matt.27:46)

"Eli, Eli, lama sabachthani? "

That is to say, My God, my God, why hast thou forsaken me? – He died broken in body and spirit.

But the words: *"it is finished"* are very important. The plan envisaged in heaven to save the fallen human race was brought to completion. Jesus saw it through to the very end. He endured and He died as a conqueror. He had done the will of his Father to the end. The plan of salvation had been accomplished.

Satan interfered with God's creation in the Garden of Eden and God could have destroyed him and Adam and Eve. But God chose to let earth's history run its course and prove Satan's deceitfulness, while making provision for those who believe to be saved by the blood of the Lamb.

After sin got a foothold in the Garden of Eden, God nearly destroyed mankind as was recorded in Genesis 6:5-7:

> *"5And GOD saw that the wickedness of man was great in the earth, and that every imagination of the thoughts of his heart was only evil continually. 6And it repented the LORD that he had made man on the earth, and it grieved him at his heart. 7And the LORD said, I will destroy man whom I have created from the face of the earth; both man, and beast, and the creeping thing, and the fowls of the air; for it repenteth me that I have made them."*

Fortunately, God observed one righteous man, namely Noah, and through him, he and his family were saved from the flood and God gave the human race another chance.

In Old Testament times, while they were still looking forward to the coming of the Messiah, they sacrificed a lamb to make atonement for their sins. This would only be fulfilled at the sacrifice of the true Lamb of God. In the same way that our faith in Jesus Christ our Redeemer will save us from eternal damnation[312], the people of the Old Testament were saved by their faith in the Messiah to come. We as sinners can not die for the sins of another. Only He who was without sin could accomplish this.

Jesus' close connection with the Jews was manifested in his words:

> **Matthew 23**
> *"37O Jerusalem, Jerusalem, thou that killest the prophets, and stonest them which are sent unto thee, how often would I have gathered thy children together, even as a hen gathereth her chickens under her wings, and ye would not!"*

The nation of Israel was chosen with regard to two issues. Firstly, they were to witness to the nations around them about the true God and obedience to his law, and secondly, that the Messiah would come from them and would witness to them firstly. They did not, however, acknowledge Jesus as the Messiah. To the contrary, they shouted out at his trial:

---

[312] 1 Jon 1:9

Matthew 27
"²³And the governor said, Why, what evil hath he done? But they cried out the more, saying, Let him be crucified. ²⁴When Pilate saw that he could prevail nothing, but that rather a tumult was made, he took water, and washed his hands before the multitude, saying, I am innocent of the blood of this just person: see ye to it. ²⁵Then answered all the people, and said, His blood be on us, and on our children."

While living amongst the Jews Jesus served them, healed them, enlightened them with his teachings, uplifting the downtrodden, especially women, children, lepers… but at his trial they shouted one and all (*²⁵Then answered all the people,*) that he should be crucified and that His blood be placed on them and their children. We are all sinners in that we fall short in obeying God's law.[313] God cannot let sin go unpunished. He is a righteous God. Yet Jesus came to earth as a lamb without blemish to die for us. Through Him we are saved. And through Jesus we are empowered to keep God's law by relying on the power of the Holy Spirit. We can be perfect if we are perfectly dependent on Jesus Christ and the Holy Spirit.[314] Jesus Christ came to live out this experience of reliance on his Father and the Holy Spirit to demonstrate that it could be done - that we can live sinless lives by relying on His power. God is a gracious God. His grace is sufficient for us. We, who believe in Jesus Christ, the Anointed One, are anxiously awaiting His return.[315]

---

[313] 1 John 1:8
[314] Matt.14:28-31

Dear Reader, if you were touched by the words of Jesus and want to know Him as your personal Savior, all you have to do is to pray with a sincere heart that God will make you aware of your sinfulness by the power of His Holy Spirit, that He will assist you to confess your sins and through your faith in Jesus Christ, the Messiah, cleanse you from your sins.

> **1 John 1**
> "⁸ *If we say that we have no sin, we deceive ourselves, and the truth is not in us.* ⁹ *If we confess our sins, he is faithful and just to forgive us [our] sins, and to cleanse us from all unrighteousness.*"

To publicly declare our faith we should then be baptized:

> **Acts 2**
> "³⁸ *Repent, and be baptized every one of you in the name of Jesus Christ for the remission of sins, and ye shall receive the gift of the Holy Ghost.*"

To grow spiritually you will have to get to know God better by studying his Word and obeying His law.

> **1 John 1**
> ⁷ *But if we walk in the light, as he is in the light, we have fellowship one with another, and the blood of Jesus Christ his Son cleanseth us from all sin.*

---

[315] Hebr.9:27,28; Rev.22:20

1 John 2
"3 And hereby we do know that we know him, if we keep his commandments. 4 He that saith, I know him, and keepeth not his commandments, is a liar, and the truth is not in him. 5 But whoso keepeth his word, in him verily is the love of God perfected: hereby know we that we are in him."

We are not saved by our good works. Our good works will be the natural outflow of our faith in Jesus Christ.

Ephesians 2
"8For by grace are ye saved through faith; and that not of yourselves: [it is] the gift of God: 9 Not of works, lest any man should boast. 10 For we are his workmanship, created in Christ Jesus unto good works, which God hath before ordained that we should walk in them."

Annexure A

A Biblical view of the state of the dead

The idea that a human being has a soul that can survive outside of its body came from ancient Babylonian and Egyptian mythology and was carried over into Greek mythology. This idea holds the view that a person's soul will carry on living in some form or another after the person's death.

The Bible, however, does not support this view. Jesus also underlined Biblical teaching in this regard. In Joh.14:2-3 He said:

> *"²In my Father's house are many mansions: if it were not so, I would have told you. I go to prepare a place for you. ³And if I go and prepare a place for you, I will come again, and receive you unto myself; that where I am, there ye may be also."*

Jesus here referred to his second coming as He described in Matthew 25:1-46. Jesus made it clear that when He comes again the dead will be resurrected to stand in the final judgment. See also Rev.20:11-15. It should be clear that whenever Jesus referred to Himself coming again, He was referring to his second coming or Advent as it is also known.

In the Old Testament the general belief was that when a person died, his life on earth was over.[316] Accordingly Psalm 115:17 states:

> "[17]The dead praise not the LORD, neither any that go down into silence..."

Those who have died are therefore not able to praise God, neither are they in heaven where such activities are going to take place in future. In the Old Testament the believer's hope was based on the coming Messiah symbolized by sacrificing the lamb without blemish – as the nation of Israel was saved from slavery in Egypt over Passover.[317] The symbol became a reality when Jesus was slain on the cross.[318]

Jesus referred to a dead person as one who is "sleeping".[319] When will this sleep end? According to 1 Thes.4:16, 17:

> "[16]For the Lord himself shall descend from heaven with a shout, with the voice of the archangel, and with the trump of God: and the dead in Christ shall rise first: [17]Then we which are alive and remain shall be caught up together with them in the clouds, to meet the Lord in the air: and so shall we ever be with the Lord."

This means that at the second coming of Jesus those who died believing in Christ as their Savior will arise first and meet Him in the clouds.[320] Those

---

[316] Ps.146:4; Eccl.9:4-6; Job 4:19-21
[317] Ex.12;5
[318] John 1:29,36; Acts 8:32; Rev.5:6; 7:10; 12:11; Isa.53:7
[319] John 11:11-14

who are still living will be changed into immortal bodies and will also be caught up in the air.

Jesus was resurrected and He is our hope for eternal live.[321] Paul describes in 1 Cor.15:39-50 that we will inherit a heavenly body after being resurrected. In verse 52 he wrote *"the dead will be raised incorruptible"* and have *"immortality"* (verse 54). Death will thus be overcome (verse 55) at the Advent of Jesus Christ.

Several people had received so-called visions of what heaven is like, for example, in a near-death experience. This does not mean, however, that they would have entered heaven directly after death, but according to the Bible they would "sleep" in their graves until Jesus returns.

Only God can give immortality.[322]

People sometimes misinterpret certain portions of Scripture and in so doing they are spreading the lie which the serpent/Satan told Eve in the Garden of Eden, when he said:

Genesis 3
"⁴And the serpent said unto the woman, Ye shall not surely die:"

But we know that Adam and Eve did not receive immortality as was also demonstrated in the time of

---

[320] 1 Thes.5:23
[321] 1 Cor.15:16-26; Acts 9:5, Luke 24:34-49
[322] 1 Tim.1:17; 1 Tim.6:13-16

the flood when everyone except those in the ark were destroyed.

> **Genesis 7**
> "*21 And all flesh died that moved upon the earth, both of fowl, and of cattle, and of beast, and of every creeping thing that creepeth upon the earth, and every man: 22All in whose nostrils was the breath of life, of all that was in the dry land, died.*"

The phrase "*22All in whose nostrils was the breath of life.*" is very important. In the same way every cell in our body needs fuel (glucose) and "spark" /oxygen to function. God gave this "breath" to Adam which caused him to be a living soul – meaning a physical body and breath. Genesis 2:7 states:

> "*7And the LORD God formed man of the dust of the ground, and breathed into his nostrils the breath of life; and man became a living soul.*"

Note that "man became a living soul", he did not receive a soul.

Peter said in his sermon during Pentecost that David did not go to heaven.[323] Jesus gave the assurance that He will give the reward to the righteous.[324] In likewise manner the ungodly will be judged when Jesus comes again.[325]

When we die our bodies decay: return to the earth - and the breath that God gave us returns to Him. We

---

[323] Acts 2:34
[324] Luke14:13,14; Rev. 22:12
[325] 2 Pet.2:9; John 5:28,29; Dan.12:12,13; Luke 12:4,5

are "switched off" like an electrical bulb without electricity.[326] There are more than 1600 references in the Bible where the words "soul" and "spirit" appear but nowhere is there any mention about the soul or spirit having immortality.

"Then shall the dust return to the earth as it was: and the spirit shall return unto God who gave it." (Eccl.12:7)

I walked in an old grave yard the other day and read on several grave stones: "Rest in peace until Jesus comes." Man would have no advantage over the animals[327] if it was not for the saving blood of Jesus, because only in believing in His redemptive blood do we have life eternal.[328]

Some Protestant churches state in their declaration of faith that they believe in Jesus Christ who ascended into heaven, sits at the right hand of God from where He will come to judge the living and the dead. This statement is according to Scripture.[329] Unfortunately, out of the other side of their mouths, these same churches assure the bereaved souls of the families that lost a loved one, the deceased person is watching them "from above". Why would Jesus come again later to judge if some (if not all who died) are in heaven already? Would heaven be

---

[326] Ps.104:29,30; Job 27:1-5
[327] Eccl.3:19,20
[328] Eph.1:7; Eph.2:8,9; 1 Pet.1:18-21
[329] 2 Tim.4:1

such a good place if we can watch our loved one's activities and trials from up there?

Others use the figurative parable of Lazarus and the rich man (Luke 16:19-31) to prove the continuation of life directly after death. Jesus did not intend to contradict Scripture by telling this story. He used the belief of the Sadducees (meet them where they are) to drive home the idea that even if it was possible for people to communicate from the grave, they would still not change their mind set. The main aim of this parable is thus to illustrate that our future destiny is decided by the choices we make in this life. Jesus criticized the Jews for the importance they gave to the traditions of men.[330]

The Biblical view on the state of the dead can thus be summarized:

- When a person dies he ceases to exist but "sleeps" in his grave.
- When Jesus returns at his second coming those who died having faith in Him will be resurrected to join Him in the clouds.
- Those still living at Jesus' second coming, who are covered by his blood, will be changed in an instant, to also meet Him in the clouds.
- Those living who rejected Jesus Christ as their Savior will be destroyed. After a thousand years Jesus will return to the earth to resurrect and to judge those inhabitants who turned their backs

---

[330] Mark 7:13

on Him (Rev.20:7-15). They will be sentenced to be destroyed in the eternal fire – eternal meaning the fire will not be quenched but will burn until everything is destroyed.[331] We read that Sodom and Gomorrah were also destroyed by an eternal fire.[332] Are they still burning today? It will be as if those who were judged never lived. They and their memory will be totally eliminated.
- After judgment the saved will live eternally in heaven in the presence of God.[333]

---

[331] Mal.4:1-3
[332] 2 Pet.2:6; Jude 1:7
[333] Rev.22:1-5

Made in the USA
Columbia, SC
26 November 2022